EDITOR: Maryanne Blacker

FOOD EDITOR: Pamela Clark

DESIGN DIRECTOR: Neil Carlyle

• • •

DESIGNER: Paula Wooller

• • •

DEPUTY FOOD EDITOR: Jan Castorina

ASSISTANT FOOD EDITOR: Kathy Snowball

ASSOCIATE FOOD EDITOR: Enid Morrison

CHIEF HOME ECONOMIST: Kathy Wharton

DEPUTY CHIEF HOME ECONOMIST:
Louise Patniotis

HOME ECONOMISTS: Sheena Chisholm,
Tracey Kern, Quinton Kohler, Jill Lange,
Alexandra McCowan, Kathy McGarry, Dimitra Stais

EDITORIAL CO-ORDINATOR: Elizabeth Hooper

KITCHEN ASSISTANT: Amy Wong

• • •

FOOD STYLISTS: Lucy Andrews,
Marie-Helene Clauzon, Rosemary de Santis,
Carolyn Fienberg

PHOTOGRAPHERS: Kevin Brown, Robert Clark,
Robert Taylor, Jon Waddy

• • •

HOME LIBRARY STAFF:

ASSISTANT EDITOR: Judy Newman

DESIGNER: Robbylee Phelan

EDITORIAL CO-ORDINATOR: Sanchia Roth

• • •

PUBLISHER: Richard Walsh

DEPUTY PUBLISHER: Graham Lawrence

ASSOCIATE PUBLISHER: Bob Neil

• • •

Produced by The Australian Women's Weekly Home Library.
Typeset by Photoset Computer Service Pty Ltd, and Letter
Perfect, Sydney. Printed by Dai Nippon Co., Ltd in Japan.
Published by Australian Consolidated Press, 54 Park Street
Sydney. Distributed by Network Distribution Company,
54 Park Street Sydney. Distributed in New Zealand by Netlink
Distribution Company (9) 302 7616. Distributed in the U.K.
by Australian Consolidated Press (UK) Ltd, (0604) 760 456.
Distributed in Canada by Whitecap Books Ltd,
(604) 9809852. Distributed in South Africa by
Intermag (011) 4933200.

• • •

The Quick-Cook Book

Includes index.

ISBN 0 949128 38 4.

1. Quick and easy cookery. I. Title.
(Series : Australian Women's Weekly
Home Library).

641.555

• • •

© A C P 1991

• • •

COVER: Chicken and Vegetable Stir-Fry, page 4. Cutlery
from Bibelot; tiles from Fred Pazotti.
OPPOSITE: Lamb with Goats' Cheese and Olives, page 55.
BACK COVER: Clockwise from top: Chick Pea and Red
Onion Salad, Cheesy Vegetable Pastries, Hot Noodles
with Spinach and Tofu, page 114.

The Quick-Cook Book

All of these deliciously easy recipes are even quicker if you organise your time, pantry and equipment. We tell you how to cook the main ingredients, and suggest accompaniments such as rice, pasta, salad and vegetables to complete a meal. Some recipes, such as main-course salads and stir-fries, often need no accompaniments. Some recipes would be suitable for snacks or light meals. Where ingredients are marinated, we have used the symbol ❖ as it is helpful to know you'll need to start preparations ahead or earlier on the day. Recipes are for 4 people, but can be easily adapted for more or less. Now turn to our pantry check list, short cuts and glossary at the back of this book.

Pamela Clark
FOOD EDITOR

BRITISH & NORTH AMERICAN READERS: Please note that conversion charts for cup and spoon measurements and oven temperatures are on page 124.

Mostly Chicken

■ *You're off to a flying start with pre-cut pieces for fuss-free preparation; they're easy to handle and cook in minutes.*

■ *Substitute one cut for another if you like; cooking time won't vary much.* ■ *You may find it handy to cook and freeze poultry pieces for an even quicker meal start.* ■ *When suitable, pound chicken fillets to an even thickness as this helps them cook evenly.* ■ *Don't overcook chicken, particularly when grilling or frying, but first seal the outside on high heat, then reduce heat to cook until tender.* ■ *In this section, we've also used spatchcocks, quail and turkey in some recipes with terrific results.* ■ *Marinated recipes are indicated by this symbol* ❖ *this means you need to start ahead of time.*

❖ SMOKED TURKEY SALAD

1 tablespoon oil
3 cloves garlic, crushed
1 teaspoon dried thyme leaves
1 teaspoon dried basil leaves
300g baby mushrooms, quartered
375g jar artichoke hearts in oil
¼ cup white wine vinegar
400g sliced smoked turkey
1 red pepper, sliced
1 yellow pepper, sliced
lettuce

Heat oil in pan, add garlic, thyme, basil and mushrooms, cook, covered, until mushrooms are soft, cool.

Drain artichokes, reserve oil. Cut artichokes in half. Combine mushroom mixture, artichokes, reserved oil and vinegar in bowl, cover, refrigerate several hours or overnight.

Cut turkey into strips. Add turkey and peppers to mushroom mixture, toss gently. Serve over lettuce in bowl.

Serves 4.

■ Recipe can be prepared a day ahead.
■ Storage: Covered, in refrigerator.
■ Freeze: Not suitable.
■ Microwave: Mushrooms suitable.

PINEAPPLE CHICKEN SALAD

3 cups (450g) sliced cooked chicken
225g can pineapple pieces, drained
1 red Spanish onion, chopped
440g can potatoes, drained, halved
1 small green cucumber, seeded, chopped
¼ cup shredded coconut
¼ cup chopped pecans or walnuts

SPICY MAYONNAISE
1 tablespoon olive oil
1 clove garlic, crushed
¼ teaspoon garam masala
¼ teaspoon ground coriander
¼ teaspoon cumin seeds
¼ teaspoon turmeric
2 egg yolks
2 teaspoons lime juice
⅓ cup olive oil, extra
2 teaspoons water

Combine all ingredients in bowl, serve topped with spicy mayonnaise.

Spicy Mayonnaise: Heat oil in pan, stir in garlic and spices, cook until bubbling; remove from heat. Blend egg yolks and juice until smooth. Add combined spice mixture and extra oil in a thin stream while motor is operating; stir in water.

Serves 4.

■ Salad and spicy mayonnaise can be made separately a day ahead.
■ Storage: Covered, in refrigerator.
■ Freeze: Not suitable.
■ Microwave: Not suitable.

RIGHT: From top: Smoked Turkey Salad, Pineapple Chicken Salad

Plates from Accoutrement

CHICKEN AND VEGETABLE STIR-FRY

4 chicken thigh fillets, sliced
⅓ cup light soy sauce
200g broccoli, chopped
2 tablespoons oil
150g green beans, sliced
1 small red pepper, sliced
1 medium (about 100g) zucchini, sliced
100g snow peas
440g can unsweetened pineapple pieces
1 tablespoon cornflour
2 tablespoons water

Combine chicken and sauce in bowl, mix well. Boil, steam or microwave broccoli until just tender, drain.

Heat oil in large pan or wok, add undrained chicken, stir-fry until lightly browned. Add beans, pepper and zucchini, stir-fry 2 minutes. Stir in broccoli, snow peas, undrained pineapple, blended cornflour and water. Stir until mixture boils and thickens slightly. Serve stir-fry with noodles or rice, if desired.

Serves 4.

■ Recipe best made just before serving.
■ Freeze: Not suitable.
■ Microwave: Broccoli suitable.

MUSTARD CHICKEN WITH SUN-DRIED TOMATOES

30g butter
4 chicken breast fillets
2 tablespoons olive oil
4 green shallots, chopped
1 clove garlic, crushed
1 tablespoon seeded mustard
¼ cup drained sun-dried tomatoes, sliced

Heat butter in pan, add chicken, cook on both sides until lightly browned, remove chicken from pan.

Heat oil in pan, add shallots, garlic, mustard and tomatoes, cook, stirring, until shallots are soft. Return chicken to pan, cook, covered, about 10 minutes or until chicken is tender. Serve with pasta or salad, if desired.

Serves 4.

■ Recipe best made just before serving.
■ Freeze: Not suitable.
■ Microwave: Not suitable.

CHICKEN WITH ROSEMARY CHILLI SAUCE

4 chicken breast fillets
plain flour
1 tablespoon oil
1 clove garlic, crushed
2 teaspoons dried rosemary leaves
½ teaspoon dried chilli flakes
1 cup water
¼ cup dry white wine
1 small chicken stock cube, crumbled
1 tablespoon cornflour
1 tablespoon light soy sauce

Toss chicken in flour; shake away excess flour. Heat oil in pan, add chicken, cook on both sides until well browned. Stir in garlic, rosemary, chilli, water, wine and stock cube. Bring to boil, simmer, covered, about 10 minutes or until chicken is tender. Remove chicken from pan.

Stir blended cornflour and sauce into pan, cook, stirring, until sauce boils and thickens. Return chicken to pan, reheat gently. Serve chicken with vegetables or salad, if desired.

Serves 4.

■ Recipe best made just before serving.
■ Freeze: Not suitable.
■ Microwave: Suitable.

CHICKEN WITH CREAMY TARRAGON SAUCE

30g butter
4 chicken breast fillets
¼ cup dry white wine
1 tablespoon brandy
250g baby mushrooms, sliced
1 cup thickened cream
1 tablespoon chopped fresh chives
1 tablespoon dried tarragon leaves

Heat butter in pan, add chicken, cook until browned and cooked through. Add wine, brandy and mushrooms to pan, cook, stirring, until mushrooms are soft. Remove chicken from pan.

Stir cream and herbs into pan, bring to boil, simmer, uncovered, about 7 minutes or until sauce is slightly thickened. Serve sauce over chicken. Serve chicken with diced fried potatoes and vegetables, rice or pasta, if desired.

Serves 4.

■ Recipe best made just before serving.
■ Freeze: Not suitable.
■ Microwave: Suitable.

LEFT: Chicken and Vegetable Stir-Fry.
ABOVE: Clockwise from left: Mustard Chicken with Sun-Dried Tomatoes, Chicken with Creamy Tarragon Sauce, Chicken with Rosemary Chilli Sauce.

Left: China from Royal Doulton

CHEESY CRUMBED CHICKEN

⅓ cup grated parmesan cheese
1½ cups (100g) stale breadcrumbs
1 tablespoon chopped fresh chives
1 tablespoon chopped fresh parsley
1 teaspoon garlic salt
4 chicken breast fillets
plain flour
1 egg, lightly beaten
½ cup milk
oil for shallow-frying
40g butter, melted
2 tablespoons lemon juice

Combine cheese, crumbs, herbs and salt in shallow dish. Place chicken between sheets of plastic wrap, flatten gently with meat mallet. Toss chicken in flour, shake away excess flour, dip in combined egg and milk, toss in crumb mixture, press crumbs on firmly.

Shallow-fry chicken in hot oil until browned and tender; drain. Pour combined butter and juice over chicken. Serve with vegetables or salad, if desired.

Serves 4.
■ Recipe can be prepared a day ahead.
■ Storage: Covered, in refrigerator.
■ Freeze: Crumbed chicken suitable.
■ Microwave: Not suitable.

WARM CHICKEN AND CORIANDER SALAD

1 tablespoon oil
¼ cup slivered almonds
6 chicken thigh fillets, sliced
1 tablespoon chopped fresh coriander
1 red pepper, chopped
2 sticks celery, chopped
12 cherry tomatoes, halved
1 avocado, chopped
3 green shallots, chopped
lettuce

DRESSING
⅓ cup mayonnaise
⅓ cup sour cream
2 tablespoons lemon juice

Heat oil in pan, add nuts, stir-fry until lightly browned, remove from pan. Reheat oil, add chicken, cook, stirring, until tender, drain on absorbent paper. Combine nuts, chicken, coriander, pepper, celery and dressing, gently stir in tomatoes, avocado and shallots; serve with lettuce.
Dressing: Combine all ingredients in bowl; mix well.

Serves 4.
■ Recipe can be prepared a day ahead and served cold.
■ Storage: Covered, in refrigerator.
■ Freeze: Not suitable.
■ Microwave: Not suitable.

SPINACH FETTUCINE WITH CREAMY CHICKEN

2 tablespoons olive oil
4 chicken breast fillets, sliced
1 onion, sliced
1 clove garlic, crushed
1 red pepper, chopped
425g can tomato puree
¼ cup grated parmesan cheese
2 tablespoons shredded fresh basil
½ teaspoon castor sugar
¼ cup sour cream
500g spinach fettucine pasta
2 tablespoons slivered almonds

Heat oil in pan, add chicken, onion, garlic and pepper, cook, stirring, about 5 minutes or until chicken is cooked through. Stir in puree, cheese, basil and sugar, bring to boil, add cream; reheat.

Meanwhile, add pasta to large pan of boiling water, boil, uncovered, until just tender; drain. Serve pasta with creamy chicken, sprinkled with almonds. Serve with salad, if desired.

Serves 4.
■ Recipe best made just before serving.
■ Freeze: Not suitable.
■ Microwave: Pasta suitable.

LEFT: From top: Cheesy Crumbed Chicken, Warm Chicken and Coriander Salad.
ABOVE: Spinach Fettucine with Creamy Chicken.

7

❖❖ COQ AU VIN KEBABS

8 chicken thigh fillets
2 bacon rashers
8 baby onions
16 (about 160g) baby mushrooms
1 teaspoon cornflour
1 tablespoon water

MARINADE
1 cup dry red wine
2 tablespoons tomato paste
2 cloves garlic, crushed
½ teaspoon dried mixed herbs
1 small chicken stock cube, crumbled

Cut chicken into 3cm pieces. Combine chicken and marinade in bowl, cover, refrigerate several hours or overnight.

Drain chicken; reserve marinade. Cut bacon into 16 pieces. Thread chicken onto 8 skewers, threading an onion into centre of each skewer. Thread a baby mushroom and piece of bacon onto each end of each skewer.

Grill or barbecue kebabs until cooked through, turning occasionally.

Heat reserved marinade in pan, stir in blended cornflour and water, stir over heat until mixture boils and thickens; strain. Serve kebabs with sauce. Serve with rice and salad, if desired.

Marinade: Combine all ingredients in bowl; mix well.

Serves 4.

■ Kebabs can be prepared a day ahead.
■ Storage: Covered, in refrigerator.
■ Freeze: Marinated chicken suitable.
■ Microwave: Not suitable.

CHICKEN WITH PROSCIUTTO AND LEMON CHIVE SAUCE

4 chicken breast fillets
4 slices prosciutto
1 small red pepper, sliced
plain flour
1 egg, lightly beaten
1 tablespoon milk
¾ cup packaged breadcrumbs
1 teaspoon dried oregano leaves
1 teaspoon dried thyme leaves
1 teaspoon paprika
2 tablespoons oil

LEMON CHIVE SAUCE
300ml carton thickened cream
½ cup sour cream
2 tablespoons lemon juice
2 teaspoons cornflour
1 tablespoon water
2 tablespoons chopped fresh chives

Cut a pocket in each fillet, gently push a slice of prosciutto and some of the red pepper in each pocket.

Toss chicken in flour, shake away excess flour. Dip chicken into combined egg and milk, toss in combined breadcrumbs, herbs and paprika.

Heat oil in pan, add chicken, cook on both sides until lightly browned and tender, drain on absorbent paper. Serve chicken with warm lemon chive sauce.

Serve with vegetables, if desired.

Lemon Chive Sauce: Combine creams and juice in pan, bring to boil, stir in blended cornflour and water, stir until mixture boils and thickens, stir in chives.

Serves 4.

- Recipe best made just before serving.
- Freeze: Filled chicken suitable.
- Microwave: Sauce suitable.

❖ GARLIC SPICED CHICKEN WITH SAFFRON RICE

8 chicken drumsticks

MARINADE
3 cloves garlic, crushed
1 tablespoon grated fresh ginger
2 teaspoons ground cardamom
1 teaspoon ground nutmeg
1 teaspoon sambal oelek
2 tablespoons lime juice

SAFFRON RICE
6 cups water
1 small chicken stock cube, crumbled
1 cup long-grain rice
pinch ground saffron

Make 3 shallow cuts on each side of each drumstick. Combine drumsticks and marinade in bowl, cover, refrigerate several hours or overnight.

Grill or barbecue drumsticks until browned and cooked through; serve with saffron rice and salad or vegetables, if desired.

Marinade: Combine all ingredients in bowl; mix well.

Saffron Rice: Bring water and stock cube to boil in pan, add rice and saffron, boil, uncovered, about 10 minutes or until just tender; drain.

Serves 4.

- Chicken can be prepared a day ahead.
- Storage: Covered, in refrigerator.
- Freeze: Marinated chicken suitable.
- Microwave: Not suitable.

CHICKEN WITH SHERRY MUSHROOM SAUCE

1 tablespoon oil
4 chicken breast fillets
20g butter
250g baby mushrooms, sliced
4 green shallots, chopped
1/3 cup dry sherry
1/3 cup water
1 small chicken stock cube, crumbled
1/3 cup cream

Heat oil in pan, add chicken, cook until browned and tender; drain on absorbent paper. Heat butter in clean pan, add mushrooms and shallots, cook, stirring, until mushrooms are tender. Stir in sherry, water, stock cube and cream. Bring to boil, simmer, uncovered until sauce thickens slightly. Add chicken, cook until heated through. Serve with vegetables, rice or pasta, if desired.

Serves 4.

- Recipe can be made a day ahead.
- Storage: Covered, in refrigerator.
- Freeze: Not suitable.
- Microwave: Not suitable.

ABOVE LEFT: From top: Chicken with Prosciutto and Lemon Chive Sauce, Coq au Vin Kebabs.
RIGHT: From top: Garlic Spiced Chicken with Saffron Rice, Chicken with Sherry Mushroom Sauce.

Left: Plates from Lifestyle Imports; basket from Appley Hoare Antiques

CHICKEN PASTA SALAD WITH VEGETABLES

200g pasta shells
250g broccoli, chopped
2 cups (300g) chopped cooked chicken
250g punnet cherry tomatoes
½ red pepper, chopped
6 green shallots, chopped
½ cup black olives
275g jar artichoke hearts in oil, drained, halved

DRESSING
¼ cup olive oil
½ cup mayonnaise
¼ cup red wine vinegar
1 teaspoon sugar
1 tablespoon chopped fresh basil
2 teaspoons chopped fresh chives

Add pasta to large pan of boiling water, boil, uncovered, until just tender; drain. Boil, steam or microwave broccoli until just tender, rinse under cold water; drain.

Combine pasta, broccoli, chicken, tomatoes, pepper, shallots, olives and artichokes in bowl; add dressing, toss well.

Dressing: Combine all ingredients in jar, shake well.

Serves 4.

■ Recipe best made just before serving.
■ Storage: Covered, in refrigerator.
■ Freeze: Not suitable.
■ Microwave: Pasta and broccoli suitable.

10

CRISPY POTATO-TOPPED CHICKEN

1 egg, lightly beaten
1 tablespoon chopped fresh chives
1 tablespoon chopped fresh parsley
1 teaspoon celery salt
3 medium (about 450g) potatoes, grated
4 chicken breast fillets
plain flour
1 egg, lightly beaten, extra,
2 tablespoons oil

Combine egg, chives, parsley, salt and potatoes in bowl. Place chicken fillets between sheets of plastic wrap, flatten gently with meat mallet. Toss chicken in flour, shake away excess flour, dip into extra egg. Heat oil in pan, add chicken, cook until browned. Spoon potato mixture evenly on top of chicken in pan, carefully turn chicken, cook until potato is well browned and crisp and chicken is cooked through. Serve chicken with vegetables or salad, if desired.

Serves 4.

■ Recipe best made just before serving.
■ Freeze: Not suitable.
■ Microwave: Not suitable.

CHICKEN IN RED WINE AND TOMATO SAUCE

30g butter
2 tablespoons olive oil
2 onions, sliced
2 cloves garlic, crushed
750g chicken thigh fillets
250g mushrooms, sliced
2 x 410g cans tomatoes
¼ cup tomato paste
¼ cup dry red wine
2 teaspoons brown sugar
1 teaspoon cracked black peppercorns
¼ cup chopped fresh basil

Heat butter and oil in pan, add onions and garlic, cook, stirring, until onions are soft. Add chicken, cook until tender. Stir in mushrooms, undrained crushed tomatoes, paste, wine, sugar and pepper. Bring to boil, simmer, uncovered, until sauce has thickened slightly; stir in basil.

Serve with rice or pasta and vegetables, if desired.

Serves 4.

■ Recipe can be made a day ahead.
■ Storage: Covered, in refrigerator.
■ Freeze: Not suitable.
■ Microwave: Suitable.

WARM CHICKEN, HAM AND MUSHROOM SALAD

100g green beans, sliced
100g sliced smoked ham
40g butter
2 cloves garlic, crushed
4 chicken breast fillets
2 tablespoons olive oil
4 green shallots, chopped
125g mushrooms, finely chopped
2 tablespoons seeded mustard
lettuce
curly endive
¼ cup French dressing

Boil, steam or microwave beans until just tender, rinse under cold water; drain. Cut ham into thin strips.

Heat butter in pan, add garlic and chicken, cook chicken on both sides until browned and cooked through. Remove chicken from pan; slice thinly. Heat oil in clean pan, add shallots, mushrooms and mustard, cook, stirring, until shallots are soft. Add ham, stir until heated through.

Toss beans, lettuce and endive in dressing, serve topped with chicken and hot ham mixture.

Serves 4.

■ Recipe best made just before serving.
■ Freeze: Not suitable.
■ Microwave: Suitable.

LEFT: Clockwise from top: Chicken Pasta Salad with Vegetables, Crispy Potato-Topped Chicken, Chicken in Red Wine and Tomato Sauce.
BELOW: Warm Chicken, Ham and Mushroom Salad.

Left: Tiles from Country Floors; plates from The Bay Tree

QUAIL AND EGGPLANT SALAD

1 tablespoon olive oil
12 quail breasts
¼ cup olive oil, extra
1 medium (about 300g) eggplant,
    chopped
1 red pepper, chopped
2 green shallots, chopped
lettuce

DRESSING
1 teaspoon grated orange rind
⅓ cup orange juice
2 tablespoons balsamic vinegar
1½ teaspoons French mustard
2 tablespoons olive oil

Heat oil in pan, add quail, cook few minutes, stirring, until browned and tender; drain on absorbent paper. Heat extra oil in pan, add eggplant, cook until lightly browned and tender; drain on absorbent paper

Cut quail into strips, combine with eggplant in bowl. Gently toss in pepper, shallots, torn lettuce leaves and dressing.
Dressing: Combine all ingredients in jar; shake well.

Serves 4.

■ Recipe can be prepared 3 hours ahead and served cold.
■ Storage: Covered, in refrigerator.
■ Freeze: Not suitable.
■ Microwave: Not suitable.

SMOKED TURKEY STROGANOFF WITH PASTA

100g packaged cream cheese
⅓ cup plain yogurt
½ cup milk
20g butter
2 green shallots, chopped
100g mushrooms, sliced
1 clove garlic, crushed
1 teaspoon dried tarragon leaves
150g sliced smoked turkey roll
500g penne rigate pasta

Blend or process cheese, yogurt and milk until smooth.

Heat butter in pan, add shallots, mushrooms and garlic, cook, stirring, until mushrooms are soft. Stir in cheese mixture and tarragon, stir over heat, without boiling, until mixture is hot. Cut turkey into strips; stir into sauce.

Meanwhile, add pasta gradually to large pan of boiling water, boil, uncovered, until just tender; drain. Serve pasta topped with sauce.

Serves 4.

■ Recipe best made just before serving.
■ Freeze: Not suitable.
■ Microwave: Suitable.

◆ GARLIC PEPPER ◆ CHICKEN WINGS

12 chicken wings

MARINADE
2 tablespoons castor sugar
¼ cup white vinegar
¼ cup oil
3 cloves garlic, crushed
3 teaspoons seasoned pepper

Combine wings and marinade in bowl, cover, refrigerate 3 hours or overnight.

Drain wings, reserve marinade. Grill or barbecue wings until well browned and cooked through, turning occasionally. Brush with reserved marinade during cooking. Serve wings with salad or vegetables, if desired.
Marinade: Combine all ingredients in bowl; mix well.

Serves 4.

■ Recipe can be prepared a day ahead.
■ Storage: Covered, in refrigerator.
■ Freeze: Marinated chicken suitable.
■ Microwave: Not suitable.

LEFT: Clockwise from left: Quail and Eggplant Salad, Garlic Pepper Chicken Wings, Smoked Turkey Stroganoff with Pasta.

China from Villeroy & Boch

❖❖ TROPICAL CHICKEN KEBABS

8 chicken thigh fillets
450g can sliced pineapple
80g snow peas, halved

MARINADE
¾ cup dry white wine
½ cup teriyaki sauce
¼ cup olive oil
1 tablespoon tomato paste
1 tablespoon grated fresh ginger
1 clove garlic, crushed
½ teaspoon dried mixed herbs

Cut chicken into cubes, combine with marinade in bowl, cover, refrigerate several hours or overnight.

Drain chicken, reserve marinade. Cut pineapple slices into quarters. Thread chicken, pineapple and snow peas onto 8 large skewers.

Barbecue, grill or pan-fry kebabs, brushing with reserved marinade, until well browned all over. Serve with rice and salad, if desired.

Marinade: Combine all ingredients in bowl; mix well.

Serves 4.

■ Recipe can be prepared a day ahead.
■ Storage: Covered, in refrigerator.
■ Freeze: Not suitable.
■ Microwave: Not suitable.

CORIANDER AND SESAME CHICKEN

100g butter
2 tablespoons chopped fresh coriander
4 chicken breast fillets
plain flour
1 egg, lightly beaten
1 tablespoon milk
½ cup sesame seeds
2 tablespoons oil

Beat butter and coriander in small bowl until well combined. Cut pocket in side of each fillet, fill with butter mixture, cover chicken, freeze 5 minutes.

Toss chicken in flour, shake away excess flour, dip in combined egg and milk, coat in sesame seeds, press seeds on firmly. Heat oil in pan, add chicken, cook until browned and cooked through. Serve with salad or vegetables, if desired.

Serves 4.

■ Recipe can be prepared a day ahead.
■ Storage: Covered, in refrigerator.
■ Freeze: Uncooked prepared chicken suitable.
■ Microwave: Not suitable.

❖❖ SWEET SPICY SPATCHCOCKS

2 x 400g spatchcocks, halved
½ teaspoon paprika
1 teaspoon grated fresh ginger
2 tablespoons honey
2 tablespoons olive oil
1 clove garlic, crushed
½ teaspoon cumin seeds

WATERCRESS SALAD
1 bunch watercress
½ red pepper, sliced
¼ cup olive oil
1½ teaspoons Worcestershire sauce
1 tablespoon honey
1 tablespoon lemon juice

Combine spatchcocks with remaining ingredients in bowl, mix well, cover, refrigerate several hours or overnight.

Grill spatchcocks until cooked through. Serve with watercress salad and vegetables, if desired.

Watercress Salad: Place watercress and pepper in bowl. Combine remaining ingredients in jar, pour over watercress.

Serves 4.

■ Recipe can be prepared a day ahead.
■ Storage: Covered, in refrigerator.
■ Freeze: Marinated spatchocks suitable.
■ Microwave: Not suitable.

SPICY CHICKEN WINGS

1kg chicken wings
2 tablespoons oil
1 tablespoon grated fresh ginger
2 cloves garlic, crushed
3 green shallots, chopped
2 tablespoons light soy sauce
¼ cup hoi sin sauce
1 teaspoon hot chilli sauce
2 teaspoons castor sugar
½ cup water
2 teaspoons cornflour
2 teaspoons water, extra

Cut chicken wings into pieces at joints. Heat oil in pan or wok, add ginger and garlic, stir over heat until aromatic. Add shallots, sauces, sugar and water, stir over heat 1 minute. Add wings, cook, covered, about 15 minutes, stirring occasionally, or until wings are cooked through. Stir in blended cornflour and extra water, stir until mixture boils and thickens. Serve with salad or vegetables, if desired.

Serves 4.

■ Recipe can be made a day ahead.
■ Storage: Covered, in refrigerator.
■ Freeze: Suitable.
■ Microwave: Not suitable.

ABOVE: Sweet Spicy Spatchcocks.
RIGHT: Clockwise from top: Coriander and Sesame Chicken, Spicy Chicken Wings, Tropical Chicken Kebabs.

Right: Plates from Powder Blue

❖ CHICKEN AND BROCCOLI STIR-FRY

6 chicken thigh fillets, sliced
1/4 cup oil
1 onion, sliced
1 red pepper, sliced
250g broccoli, chopped
100g bean sprouts
2 tablespoons chopped peanuts

MARINADE
1/3 cup teriyaki marinade
2 tablespoons green ginger wine
2 cloves garlic, crushed
2 tablespoons plum sauce

Combine chicken and marinade in bowl, cover, refrigerate 3 hours or overnight.

Drain chicken from marinade, reserve marinade. Heat 2 tablespoons of the oil in large pan or wok. Add chicken in batches, stir-fry until tender, remove chicken from pan.

Heat remaining oil in pan, add onion, stir-fry until soft. Add pepper, broccoli and sprouts, stir-fry until vegetables are just tender. Return chicken and reserved marinade to pan, stir-fry until mixture is heated through. Serve sprinkled with peanuts. Serve stir-fry with rice or noodles, if desired.

Marinade: Combine all ingredients in bowl; mix well.

Serves 4.

■ Recipe can be prepared a day ahead.
■ Storage: Covered, in refrigerator.
■ Freeze: Marinated chicken suitable.
■ Microwave: Not suitable.

SPICY FRIED RICE WITH CHICKEN

1 tablespoon oil
1 onion, chopped
1 clove garlic, crushed
1 green pepper, chopped
1 red pepper, chopped
100g mushrooms, chopped
2½ cups cooked rice
1 tablespoon oyster sauce
1 tablespoon teriyaki sauce
2 teaspoons oil, extra
1 teaspoon paprika
½ teaspoon celery salt
1 teaspoon lemon pepper
1 tablespoon chilli sauce
1 cup (150g) chopped cooked chicken

Heat oil in large pan or wok, add onion, garlic, peppers and mushrooms, stir-fry until peppers are soft. Add rice, oyster and teriyaki sauces, stir-fry until rice is heated through; remove from pan, keep warm.

Meanwhile, heat extra oil in clean pan, add paprika, salt, pepper and chilli sauce, stir until bubbling, add chicken, stir until heated through. Add to rice mixture, stir-fry until combined. Serve with a green salad, if desired.

Serves 4.

- ■ Recipe best made just before serving.
- ■ Freeze: Not suitable.
- ■ Microwave: Not suitable

TURKEY AND BACON ROLLS

4 bacon rashers
4 x 150g turkey breast pieces
¼ cup oil
½ cup dry white wine
¼ cup lemon juice
1 tablespoon seeded mustard
150g baby mushrooms, sliced
3 cups (300g) bean sprouts
60g butter, chopped
4 green shallots, chopped

Wrap a bacon rasher around each turkey piece, secure with toothpick.

Heat oil in pan, add rolls, cook until browned and tender. Pour excess oil from pan. Stir in wine, juice and mustard, bring to boil, simmer, uncovered, 2 minutes. Remove rolls from pan.

Add mushrooms and sprouts to pan, cook, stirring, until mushrooms are soft, remove from heat. Whisk in butter a little at a time, stir in shallots. Serve vegetable mixture with turkey. Serve rolls with salad, if desired.

Serves 4.

- ■ Recipe best made just before serving.
- ■ Freeze: Not suitable.
- ■ Microwave: Not suitable.

LEFT: From left: Spicy Fried Rice with Chicken, Chicken and Broccoli Stir-Fry. ABOVE: Turkey and Bacon Rolls.

Left: China from Royal Doulton. Above: Cloth from Accoutrement

❖ MUSTARD AND ROSEMARY CHICKEN

8 chicken thigh fillets, halved
1/3 cup French mustard
1/4 cup seeded mustard
1/4 cup lemon juice
2/3 cup olive oil
3 cloves garlic, crushed
1 tablespoon cracked black peppercorns
1 tablespoon dried rosemary leaves
1 small chicken stock cube, crumbled
6 small (about 390g) zucchini, sliced
1 red pepper, sliced

Combine all ingredients in bowl, cover, refrigerate 3 hours or overnight.

Remove chicken from marinade, reserve marinade and vegetables. Place chicken on rack in baking dish, bake, uncovered, in hot oven about 15 minutes or until tender.

Place reserved marinade and vegetables in pan, cook, stirring, until vegetables are tender; serve with chicken. Serve with rice or noodles, if desired.

Serves 4.

■ Recipe can be prepared a day ahead.
■ Storage: Covered, in refrigerator.
■ Freeze: Marinated mixture suitable.
■ Microwave: Vegetable marinade mixture suitable.

❖ SPICY GARLIC CHICKEN

12 chicken drumsticks
2 teaspoons brown sugar
1/2 teaspoon cornflour
1/2 teaspoon water

MARINADE
3 cloves garlic, crushed
1 teaspoon grated fresh ginger
1/3 cup hoi sin sauce
2 tablespoons light soy sauce
1/4 cup dry sherry
1/4 teaspoon sambal oelek
1 teaspoon sesame oil

Combine chicken and marinade in bowl, cover, refrigerate 3 hours or overnight.

Remove chicken from marinade, reserve marinade. Grill chicken until well browned and cooked through.

Blend sugar, cornflour and water in pan, stir in reserved marinade, stir over heat until mixture boils and thickens. Serve sauce with chicken. Serve with rice or noodles and vegetables, if desired.

Marinade: Combine all ingredients in bowl; mix well.

Serves 4.

■ Chicken can be prepared a day ahead.
■ Storage: Covered, in refrigerator.
■ Freeze: Not suitable.
■ Microwave: Not suitable.

SPICY CHICKEN WITH PEPPERS

2 tablespoons oil
3 cloves garlic, crushed
2 teaspoons grated fresh ginger
1 teaspoon cumin seeds
1 teaspoon turmeric
1 teaspoon garam masala
1 teaspoon cracked black peppercorns
1 teaspoon ground coriander
1kg chicken drummettes
1 onion, sliced
1 red pepper, chopped
1 green pepper, chopped
410g can tomatoes
2 small chicken stock cubes, crumbled

Heat oil in pan, add garlic, ginger, spices, peppercorns and coriander, cook, stirring, about 1 minute or until spices are fragrant.

Add chicken, cook, stirring, until chicken is browned; add onion, cook until soft. Stir in peppers, undrained crushed tomatoes and stock cubes. Bring to boil, simmer, covered, or until chicken is cooked through. Serve chicken with rice, if desired.

Serves 4.

■ Recipe can be made a day ahead.
■ Storage: Covered, in refrigerator.
■ Freeze: Suitable.
■ Microwave: Suitable.

ABOVE: From top: Spicy Chicken with Peppers, Mustard and Rosemary Chicken. RIGHT: From left: Chicken, Fennel and Orange Salad, Spicy Garlic Chicken.

Right: Terracotta basket from The Parterre Garden; tiles from Country Floors

CHICKEN, FENNEL AND ORANGE SALAD

1 tablespoon olive oil
30g butter
4 chicken breast fillets, sliced
1 fennel bulb, thinly sliced
½ cup black olives
3 green shallots, chopped
2 oranges, segmented
lettuce

DRESSING
½ cup orange juice
2 tablespoons red wine vinegar
2 tablespoons olive oil
½ teaspoon sugar

Heat oil and butter in pan, add chicken, cook, stirring, until well browned and tender; drain.

Combine chicken, fennel, olives, shallots, oranges and dressing in bowl; toss gently. Serve chicken mixture on lettuce.

Dressing: Combine all ingredients in jar; shake well.

Serves 4.

■ Salad can be made a day ahead and served cold.
■ Storage: Covered, in refrigerator.
■ Freeze: Not suitable.
■ Microwave: Not suitable.

❖❖ CRISPY FRIED QUAIL IN SPICY MARINADE

8 quail
2 tablespoons oil
2 medium (about 400g) leeks
60g butter

MARINADE
½ cup light soy sauce
2 tablespoons castor sugar
1 teaspoon cumin seeds, crushed
½ teaspoon five spice powder
2 teaspoons grated fresh ginger
2 teaspoons sambal oelek

Cut quail into quarters. Combine quail and marinade in bowl, cover, refrigerate several hours or overnight.

Drain quail, discard marinade. Heat oil in pan, add quail, cook until well browned and cooked through.

Meanwhile, cut leeks into 5cm lengths. Heat butter in pan, add leeks, cook, covered, over low heat until leeks are soft, serve with quail. Serve with salad or vegetables, if desired.

Marinade: Combine all ingredients in bowl; mix well.

Serves 4.

■ Quail can be marinated a day ahead.
■ Storage: Covered, in refrigerator.
■ Freeze: Marinated quail suitable.
■ Microwave: Not suitable.

CREAMY CHICKEN WITH BACON AND MUSHROOMS

4 chicken thigh fillets, sliced
plain flour
¼ cup oil
1 onion, chopped
3 bacon rashers, chopped
½ cup dry white wine
1 cup hot water
1 small chicken stock cube, crumbled
150g baby mushrooms, quartered
¼ cup chopped roasted hazelnuts
1 teaspoon dried tarragon leaves
½ cup thickened cream
3 green shallots, chopped
4 bread rolls

Toss chicken in flour, shake away excess flour. Heat oil in pan, add onion and bacon, cook, stirring, until onion is soft. Add chicken, cook, stirring, until chicken is lightly browned. Stir in wine, water and stock cube, stir over heat until mixture boils. Stir in mushrooms, nuts, tarragon and cream, simmer, covered, about 5 minutes or until chicken is tender. Stir in shallots.

Slice tops from rolls, hollow out rolls, leaving 2cm shell. Heat rolls on oven tray in moderately hot oven 5 minutes. Divide hot chicken mixture between rolls. Serve rolls with salad, if desired.

Serves 4.

- Filling can be prepared a day ahead.
- Storage: Covered, in refrigerator.
- Freeze: Not suitable.
- Microwave: Not suitable.

CHILLI CHICKEN WITH CORN CHIPS

40g butter
4 chicken thigh fillets, chopped
4 green shallots, chopped
1 cup tomato puree
½ cup mild chilli sauce
1 tablespoon chopped fresh parsley
200g packet cheese-flavoured corn chips
1 cup (125g) grated tasty cheese
1 tablespoon chopped fresh parsley, extra

Heat butter in pan, add chicken, cook, stirring, until well browned. Add shallots, cook, stirring, until shallots are soft. Stir in puree, sauce and parsley, simmer about 5 minutes or until sauce is thickened.

Place chips in flameproof dish, top with chicken mixture, sprinkle with cheese. Grill until cheese is melted, serve sprinkled with extra parsley. Serve with salad, if desired.

Serves 4.

- Recipe, without chips, can be prepared a day ahead.
- Storage: Covered, in refrigerator.
- Freeze: Chicken mixture suitable.
- Microwave: Suitable.

SWEET TOMATO AND CHICKEN CURRY

¼ cup oil
1 onion, chopped
1 clove garlic, crushed
1 teaspoon grated fresh ginger
6 chicken thigh fillets, sliced
2 tablespoons curry powder
1 large (about 200g) potato, chopped
2 medium carrots, chopped
1 teaspoon sugar
425g can tomato puree
¼ cup chutney
2 tablespoons tomato paste
1½ cups water
½ cup frozen peas

Heat oil in large pan or wok, add onion, garlic and ginger, stir-fry until onion is soft. Add chicken, stir-fry until lightly browned. Add curry powder, potato and carrots, stir-fry further 2 minutes, add sugar, puree, chutney, paste, water and peas.

Bring to boil, stirring, then simmer, uncovered, until chicken and vegetables are tender and sauce is slightly thickened. Serve with rice, if desired.

Serves 4.

- Recipe can be made a day ahead.
- Storage: Covered, in refrigerator.
- Freeze: Suitable.
- Microwave: Not suitable.

LEFT: Clockwise from top: Chilli Chicken with Corn Chips, Creamy Chicken with Bacon and Mushrooms, Crispy Fried Quail in Spicy Marinade.
ABOVE: Sweet Tomato and Chicken Curry.

Left: China from Mikasa; fabric from Redelman Fabrics. Above: Plate from Mikasa

CHICKEN AND GOATS' CHEESE SALAD

100g green beans, chopped
100g snow peas
100g goats' cheese, cubed
plain flour
1 egg, lightly beaten
¼ cup packaged breadcrumbs
oil for deep-frying
1 red pepper, sliced
3 cups (450g) chopped cooked chicken
lettuce
4 green shallots, chopped

DRESSING
⅔ cup olive oil
1 tablespoon balsamic vinegar
1 tablespoon white vinegar
2 teaspoons seeded mustard
1 clove garlic, crushed

Boil, steam or microwave beans and peas separately until just tender; rinse under cold water, drain well.

Toss cheese in flour, shake away excess flour, dip into egg, toss in breadcrumbs. Deep-fry cheese cubes in hot oil until lightly browned, drain cubes on absorbent paper.

Combine beans, peas, cheese, pepper, chicken, torn lettuce and shallots in bowl, add dressing, toss gently.

Dressing: Combine all ingredients in jar; shake well.

Serves 4.

- Salad and dressing can be made separately, 3 hours ahead.
- Storage: Covered, in refrigerator.
- Freeze: Not suitable.
- Microwave: Vegetables suitable.

❖ QUAIL WITH MARINATED PIMIENTOS

410g can pimientos, drained, sliced
130g can corn kernels, drained
2 tomatoes, chopped
6 black olives, quartered
⅓ cup olive oil
¼ cup balsamic vinegar
½ teaspoon sugar
8 quail
¼ cup olive oil, extra

Combine pimientos, corn, tomatoes and olives in bowl. Stir in combined oil, vinegar and sugar, cover, refrigerate several hours or overnight.

Drain pimiento mixture; reserve mixture, discard marinade. Brush quail with extra oil, barbecue, grill or pan-fry quail until browned and tender. Serve quail with reserved pimiento mixture. Serve with salad or vegetables, if desired.

Serves 4.

- ■ Pimientos can be made a day ahead. Quail best cooked just before serving.
- ■ Storage: Pimientos, covered, in refrigerator.
- ■ Freeze: Not suitable.
- ■ Microwave: Not suitable.

CHICKEN WITH SPICY PEANUT SAUCE

30g butter
1 tablespoon oil
4 chicken breast fillets
2 teaspoons chopped fresh coriander

SPICY PEANUT SAUCE
1 tablespoon oil
1 small onion, chopped
1 teaspoon curry powder
½ teaspoon sambal oelek
⅓ cup crunchy peanut butter
1 small chicken stock cube, crumbled
⅔ cup water
150g can coconut milk
2 teaspoons brown sugar
2 teaspoons light soy sauce

Heat butter and oil in pan, add chicken, cook until browned and tender. Serve chicken with spicy peanut sauce, sprinkle with coriander. Serve with rice, salad or vegetables, if desired.
Spicy Peanut Sauce: Heat oil in pan, add onion, curry powder and sambal oelek, cook, stirring, until onion is soft. Stir in peanut butter, stock cube, water, milk, sugar and sauce. Bring to boil, simmer, uncovered, until slightly thickened.

Serves 4.

- ■ Chicken best cooked just before serving. Sauce can be made a day ahead.
- ■ Storage: Sauce, covered, in refrigerator.
- ■ Freeze: Sauce suitable.
- ■ Microwave: Sauce suitable.

CITRUS CHICKEN

40g butter
4 chicken breast fillets, sliced
1 teaspoon grated lemon rind
1 teaspoon grated orange rind
2 teaspoons white vinegar
1 teaspoon castor sugar
1 teaspoon brandy
1 teaspoon cornflour
½ cup orange juice
1 orange, segmented
2 medium (about 400g) leeks

Heat butter in pan, add chicken, cook, stirring, until chicken is browned. Add rinds, vinegar, sugar, brandy and blended cornflour and juice, stir over heat until mixture boils and thickens. Stir in orange segments, stir gently until heated through.

Meanwhile, cut leeks in half lengthways. Boil, steam or microwave leeks until tender. Place leeks on plate, top with chicken mixture. Serve with vegetables, if desired.

Serves 4.

- ■ Recipe best made just before serving.
- ■ Freeze: Not suitable.
- ■ Microwave: Suitable.

*LEFT: From top: Quail with Marinated Pimientos, Chicken and Goats' Cheese Salad.
BELOW: From top: Chicken with Spicy Peanut Sauce, Citrus Chicken.*

Below: Plates from Accoutrement; tiles from Country Floors

Beef

■ *Quickest would be steak with caviar butter or blue cheese butter (these are great to keep on hand in the freezer), or go for our super burger with the lot!* ■ *The key to short-cut cooking is to use tender cuts of steak and good quality mince; both give top results quickly without losing flavour or tenderness.* ■ *You don't have to use the steak we specify in recipes; substitute the one you prefer.* ■ *Partly-frozen beef is easier to slice, but make sure it is thawed before beginning to cook.* ■ *Always cook beef over a high heat at first to seal the outside before continuing the recipe; beef will be tough and dry if you overcook it.* ■ *Marinated recipes are indicated by this symbol* ❖ *this means you will have to start ahead of time.*

❖ BEEF AND VEGETABLE STIR-FRY

350g rump steak
1 tablespoon oil
1 green pepper, chopped
300g green beans, chopped
200g baby mushrooms, halved
¼ cup water
⅓ cup roasted unsalted cashews

MARINADE
¼ cup soy sauce
2 tablespoons hoi sin sauce
⅓ cup plum sauce
1 teaspoon sesame oil
2 tablespoons dry white wine
3 teaspoons cornflour
2 teaspoons grated fresh ginger
1 clove garlic, crushed

Cut steak into thin slices. Combine steak with marinade in bowl, cover, refrigerate several hours or overnight.

Heat oil in large pan or wok, add undrained steak mixture and vegetables, stir-fry until steak is lightly browned. Add water, bring to boil, simmer, covered, few minutes or until vegetables are tender. Serve sprinkled with nuts. Serve with rice or noodles, if desired.

Marinade: Combine all ingredients in bowl; mix well.
Serves 4.
■ Recipe can be prepared a day ahead.
■ Storage: Covered, in refrigerator.
■ Freeze: Not suitable.
■ Microwave: Not suitable.

❖ PIQUANT GRILLED STEAKS

4 T-bone steaks

MARINADE
¼ cup light soy sauce
2 tablespoons oyster sauce
1 tablespoon hoi sin sauce
1 tablespoon brown sugar
1 tablespoon dry sherry
1 clove garlic, crushed
1 teaspoon sesame oil

Place steaks in dish, pour over marinade; cover, refrigerate 3 hours or overnight.

Drain steaks, reserve marinade. Grill steaks until done as desired, brushing with reserved marinade during cooking. Serve with vegetables or salad, if desired.
Marinade: Combine all ingredients in bowl; mix well.
Serves 4.

■ Steaks can be marinated a day ahead.
■ Storage: Covered, in refrigerator.
■ Freeze: Marinated steaks suitable.
■ Microwave: Not suitable.

RIGHT: From top: Piquant Grilled Steaks, Beef and Vegetable Stir-Fry.

Plates and wooden mat from Country Floors; cloth from Accoutrement

TO TEST IF STEAK IS DONE
It can be difficult to determine the stage at which steak is ready for serving; experience is the best teacher. Steak cooked to the rare stage is quite spongy and soft to the touch. Medium rare is less spongy and so on. From left: fillet steak well done, medium rare and rare.

RISSOLES WITH CREAMY NOODLES

1kg minced beef
2 tablespoons chopped fresh mint
1 onion, grated
1 egg, lightly beaten
1 clove garlic, crushed
1 small beef stock cube, crumbled
¾ cup stale breadcrumbs
2 tablespoons oil

CREAMY NOODLES
85g packet 2 Minute Noodles Beef
 Flavour
300ml carton cream
1 green shallot, chopped

Combine mince, mint, onion, egg, garlic, stock cube and breadcrumbs in bowl. Divide mixture into 8 portions, shape into rissoles. Heat oil in pan, cook rissoles on both sides until well browned and cooked through. Serve rissoles with creamy noodles, salad or vegetables, if desired.
Creamy Noodles: Add noodles to pan of boiling water, boil, uncovered, 2 minutes, drain. Return noodles to pan, add flavour sachet and cream, stir over heat 1 minute, stir in shallot.

Serves 4.

- ■ Rissoles can be made a day ahead.
- ■ Storage: Covered, in refrigerator.
- ■ Freeze: Rissoles suitable.
- ■ Microwave: Noodles suitable.

STEAKS WITH BLUE CHEESE BUTTER

2 tablespoons oil
4 sirloin steaks
2 tablespoons chopped fresh parsley

BLUE CHEESE BUTTER
75g soft blue vein cheese
60g butter, softened

Heat oil in pan, cook steaks until done as desired. Serve steaks with blue cheese butter, sprinkled with parsley. Serve with vegetables or salad, if desired.
Blue Cheese Butter: Beat cheese and butter in small bowl until well combined. Spoon mixture onto foil, roll foil around mixture to form a log, freeze until firm.

Serves 4.

- ■ Butter can be made a week ahead.
- ■ Storage: Covered, in refrigerator.
- ■ Freeze: Butter suitable.
- ■ Microwave: Not suitable.

BEEF SAUSAGES WITH BACON AND MUSTARD CREAM

½ cup chopped dried apricots
½ cup chopped pistachios
1 tablespoon chopped fresh parsley
8 thick beef sausages
8 bacon rashers
1 tablespoon oil

MUSTARD CREAM
⅔ cup thickened cream, whipped
1 teaspoon Worcestershire sauce
2 teaspoons seeded mustard
1 small red pepper, chopped

Combine apricots, nuts and parsley in bowl. Make a shallow cut lengthways down centre of sausages, fill with apricot mixture. Wrap bacon rashers around sausages, secure with toothpicks.

Heat oil in pan, add sausages, cook until lightly browned all over. Place sausages on rack in baking dish, bake, uncovered, in moderate oven about 10 minutes or until cooked through. Serve sausages with mustard cream. Serve with salad or vegetables, if desired.
Mustard Cream: Combine all ingredients in small bowl; mix well.

Serves 4.

- ■ Mustard cream and sausages can be prepared a day ahead.
- ■ Storage: Separately, covered, in refrigerator.
- ■ Freeze: Uncooked filled sausages suitable.
- ■ Microwave: Not suitable.

STEAKS WITH CAVIAR BUTTER

50g butter, softened
2 teaspoons red lumpfish roe (caviar)
½ teaspoon seasoned pepper
4 beef eye-fillet steaks
1 tablespoon oil
½ cup dry red wine
2 tablespoons chopped fresh chives
1 tablespoon red lumpfish roe
 (caviar), extra
1 teaspoon cornflour
1 tablespoon water

Beat butter, roe and pepper in small bowl until well combined. Spoon mixture onto foil, roll foil around mixture to form a log, freeze until firm.

Cut butter into 4 slices. Cut a pocket in each steak, insert a slice of butter in each pocket. Heat oil in pan, add steaks, cook until done as desired, remove from pan.

Add wine, chives, extra roe and blended cornflour and water to same pan, cook, stirring, until mixture boils and thickens. Serve sauce over steaks. Serve with vegetables or salad, if desired.

Serves 4.

- ■ Butter can be made a week ahead.
- ■ Storage: Covered, in refrigerator.
- ■ Freeze: Butter suitable.
- ■ Microwave: Not suitable.

LEFT: Rissoles with Creamy Noodles.
RIGHT: Clockwise from left: Steaks with Blue Cheese Butter, Beef Sausages with Bacon and Mustard Cream, Steaks with Caviar Butter.

Left: Plates from Home and Garden; cloth from Mosmania; tiles from Country Floors. Right: China from Wedgwood Waterford; fabric from Redelman Fabrics

PEPPERED STEAKS WITH ZUCCHINI

1 tablespoon seasoned pepper
4 beef rib-eye steaks
1 tablespoon oil
20g butter
2 cloves garlic, crushed
2 green zucchini, sliced
2 yellow zucchini, sliced
1 tablespoon chopped fresh basil
½ teaspoon dried rosemary leaves
1 teaspoon seeded mustard
20g butter, extra
1 tablespoon dry sherry
2 tablespoons cream

Press pepper onto steaks. Heat oil and butter in pan, add steaks, cook until done as desired; remove from pan.

Add garlic and zucchini to pan, cook, stirring, until zucchini are just tender. Stir in herbs, mustard, extra butter and sherry, bring to boil, stir in cream. Serve sauce over steaks. Serve with salad or vegetables, if desired.

Serves 4.

- Recipe best made just before serving.
- Freeze: Not suitable.
- Microwave: Not suitable.

STEAKS WITH MUSHROOM SAUCE

50g butter
250g large flat mushrooms, chopped
1 onion, chopped
2 tablespoons plain flour
¾ cup water
½ cup dry red wine
1 large beef stock cube, crumbled
4 New York-style steaks
1 tablespoon chopped fresh parsley

Heat butter in pan, add mushrooms and onion, cook, stirring, until onion is soft. Add flour, cook, stirring, 1 minute. Stir in water, wine and stock cube, stir over heat until sauce boils and thickens, simmer, uncovered, 10 minutes.

Meanwhile, grill steaks until done as desired. Stir half the parsley into sauce, serve over steaks, sprinkle with remaining parsley. Serve with vegetables or salad, if desired.

Serves 4.

- Steak best cooked just before serving. Sauce can be made a day ahead.
- Storage: Covered, in refrigerator.
- Freeze: Not suitable.
- Microwave: Sauce suitable.

BEEF AND LEEK KEBABS WITH HUMMUS

500g minced beef
1 cup (70g) stale breadcrumbs
1 teaspoon dried rosemary leaves
2 teaspoons grated lemon rind
2 small beef stock cubes, crumbled
¼ teaspoon garlic powder
1 egg, lightly beaten
1 medium (about 200g) leek
1 tablespoon olive oil
pinch paprika

HUMMUS
425g can garbanzos (chick peas), rinsed, drained
1 clove garlic, crushed
½ cup olive oil
¼ cup lemon juice

Combine mince, breadcrumbs, rosemary, rind, stock cubes, garlic powder and egg in bowl; mix well. Shape mixture into 24 sausage shapes. Cut leek into 12 thick pieces. Thread sausage shapes and leek onto 12 skewers.

Brush kebabs with oil, grill or barbecue until cooked through. Serve kebabs with hummus sprinkled with paprika. Serve with salad or vegetables, if desired.

Hummus: Blend or process all ingredients until smooth.

Serves 4.

- Recipe can be prepared a day ahead.
- Storage: Covered, in refrigerator.
- Freeze: Kebabs suitable.
- Microwave: Not suitable.

LEFT: Peppered Steaks with Zucchini.
RIGHT: From top: Steaks with Mushroom Sauce, Beef and Leek Kebabs with Hummus.

Left: China from Villeroy & Boch; napkin from Home and Garden

SCOTCH FILLET STEAKS WITH RED PEPPER BUTTER

1 tablespoon oil
4 Scotch fillet steaks

RED PEPPER BUTTER
1 red pepper
125g butter
1 tablespoon chopped fresh chives
½ teaspoon cracked black
  peppercorns

Heat oil in large pan, add steaks, cook until done as desired. Serve steaks topped with red pepper butter. Serve with vegetables or salad, if desired.
Red Pepper Butter: Quarter pepper, remove seeds and membrane. Grill pepper, skin side up, until skin blisters and blackens. Peel skin from pepper, chop pepper finely. Beat butter in small bowl, stir in pepper, chives and peppercorns.

Serves 4.
■ Butter can be made a week ahead.
■ Storage: Covered, in refrigerator.
■ Freeze: Butter suitable.
■ Microwave: Not suitable.

❖ DOUBLE-FRIED BEEF
❖ WITH PINEAPPLE SAUCE

750g rump steak
¼ cup teriyaki marinade
cornflour
oil for deep-frying

PINEAPPLE SAUCE
2 teaspoons oil
½ teaspoon sesame oil
1 onion, chopped
1 red pepper, chopped
4 green shallots, chopped
1 tablespoon grated fresh ginger
225g can sweetened pineapple
    pieces, drained
2 teaspoons soy sauce
1¼ cups water
1 small chicken stock cube, crumbled
2 teaspoons cornflour
2 teaspoons water, extra

Cut steak into thin strips, combine with teriyaki marinade in bowl, cover, refrigerate several hours or overnight.

Drain steak from marinade, discard marinade. Toss steak in cornflour, shake away excess cornflour. Deep-fry steak in hot oil in batches until tender. Drain on absorbent paper.

Reheat oil, deep-fry steak again until crisp, serve with pineapple sauce. Serve with rice, if desired.

Pineapple Sauce: Heat oils in pan, add onion, pepper and shallots, cook, stirring, until onion is soft. Add ginger, pineapple, sauce, water, stock cube and blended cornflour and extra water, stir until mixture boils and thickens, simmer 2 minutes.

Serves 4.

- Recipe can be prepared a day ahead.
- Storage: Covered, in refrigerator.
- Freeze: Not suitable.
- Microwave: Sauce suitable.

❖ STEAKS WITH PORT
❖ AND PEARS

425g can pear halves in syrup
⅓ cup port
1 clove garlic, crushed
2 teaspoons chopped fresh chives
1 teaspoon grated lemon rind
4 beef eye-fillet steaks
20g butter
1 tablespoon oil
1 small beef stock cube, crumbled
⅓ cup water
2 teaspoons cornflour
2 teaspoons water, extra
1 tablespoon chopped fresh
    chives, extra

Drain pears, reserve half a cup syrup. Combine reserved syrup, port, garlic, chives and rind in bowl, add steaks, cover, refrigerate several hours or overnight.

Remove steaks from marinade, pat steaks dry with absorbent paper, reserve marinade.

Heat butter and oil in pan, add steaks, cook on both sides few minutes until well browned. Add marinade, stock cube and water, bring to boil, simmer, covered, about 10 minutes or until steaks are tender; remove from pan.

Strain pan juices, return juices to pan, add blended cornflour and extra water, stir over heat until sauce boils and thickens. Add 4 pear halves to pan, reserve remaining pear halves for another use. Stir gently over heat until pear halves are warmed through. Serve steaks with sauce and pears, sprinkle with extra chives. Serve with vegetables, if desired.

Serves 4.

- Recipe can be prepared a day ahead.
- Freeze: Not suitable.
- Microwave: Not suitable.

LEFT: From top: Scotch Fillet Steaks with Red Pepper Butter, Double Fried Beef with Pineapple Sauce.
BELOW: Steaks with Port and Pears.

Left: Plates from Home and Garden; tiles from Country Floors. Below: China from Wedgwood

GRILLED STEAKS WITH CREAMY CORIANDER SAUCE

4 sirloin steaks

CREAMY CORIANDER SAUCE
½ teaspoon cornflour
½ cup buttermilk
½ cup sour cream
1 clove garlic, crushed
2 teaspoons chopped fresh coriander
1 teaspoon grated lime rind
2 teaspoons lime juice

Grill or barbecue steaks until cooked as desired; serve with creamy coriander sauce. Serve with vegetables or salad, if desired.

Creamy Coriander Sauce: Blend cornflour with a little of the buttermilk, add to pan with remaining ingredients. Stir over heat until sauce boils and thickens.

Serves 4.

- Sauce can be made a day ahead.
- Storage: Covered, in refrigerator.
- Freeze: Not suitable.
- Microwave: Sauce suitable.

HERBED PATTIES WITH CURRY SAUCE

500g minced beef
1 cup (70g) stale breadcrumbs
⅓ cup packaged breadcrumbs
1 egg, lightly beaten
2 tablespoons chopped fresh coriander
½ teaspoon sambal oelek
1 tablespoon oil
2 tablespoons oil, extra
1 onion, chopped
1 tablespoon curry powder
410g can tomatoes
1 tablespoon tomato paste
2 teaspoons sugar

Combine beef, both breadcrumbs, egg, coriander and sambal oelek in bowl; mix well. Shape mixture into 12 patties.

Heat oil in large pan, add patties, cook until cooked through; remove from pan.

Heat extra oil in pan, add onion and curry powder, cook, stirring, until onion is soft. Add undrained crushed tomatoes, paste and sugar, bring to boil, return patties to pan, simmer, uncovered, until sauce is thickened slightly. Serve with rice or pasta, if desired.

Serves 4.

- Recipe can be prepared a day ahead.
- Storage: Covered, in refrigerator.
- Freeze: Patties suitable.
- Microwave: Not suitable.

SAUSAGE AND BEAN HOT POT

500g thin beef sausages
1 teaspoon oil
1 onion, sliced
2 tablespoons plain flour
1 small beef stock cube, crumbled
1 cup water
440g can baked beans
2 tablespoons tomato paste
410g can tomatoes
1 tablespoon chopped fresh parsley
1 teaspoon seasoned pepper
1 tablespoon chopped fresh parsley, extra

Prick sausages with fork. Heat oil in pan, add sausages, cook until well browned all over, drain on absorbent paper.

Add onion to same pan, cook, stirring, until onion is soft. Add flour, cook, stirring, 1 minute. Add stock cube and water, stir until mixture boils and thickens slightly.

Cut sausages in half, add to pan with undrained beans, paste, undrained crushed tomatoes, parsley and pepper, stir until heated through. Serve sprinkled with extra parsley. Serve hot pot with salad or vegetables, if desired.

Serves 4.

- Recipe can be prepared a day ahead.
- Storage: Covered, in refrigerator.
- Freeze: Not suitable.
- Microwave: Suitable .

ABOVE: Sausage and Bean Hot Pot.
RIGHT: From back: Herbed Patties with Curry Sauce, Grilled Steaks with Creamy Coriander Sauce.

Above: China from Wedgwood. Right: Plates from The Bay Tree; tiles from Country Floors

GARLIC MUSTARD STEAK SALAD

2 cloves garlic, crushed
1kg piece rump steak
2 tablespoons oil
1 carrot
1 small green cucumber, seeded
1 red Spanish onion, sliced

DRESSING
½ cup oil
¼ cup white vinegar
1 tablespoon chopped fresh parsley
1 tablespoon seeded mustard
1 teaspoon castor sugar

Rub garlic over both sides of steak. Heat oil in pan, add steak, cook until done as desired. Remove steak from pan. Cut steak into strips, reserve any juices.

Cut carrot and cucumber into strips. Place onion in bowl, cover with boiling water, stand 5 minutes; drain.

Combine steak, reserved juices, carrot, cucumber, onion and dressing in bowl.

Dressing: Combine all ingredients in jar; shake well.

Serves 4.

- Salad can be made several hours ahead.
- Storage: Covered, in refrigerator.
- Freeze: Not suitable.
- Microwave: Not suitable.

BEEF KEBABS WITH MUSTARD MARINADE

400g piece rump steak
8 gherkins
2 teaspoons cornflour
¼ cup water

MUSTARD MARINADE
¼ cup drained, sun-dried tomatoes, sliced
1 teaspoon sugar
1 tablespoon seeded mustard
½ cup dry white wine

Cut steak into 2cm cubes, cut gherkins into 2cm lengths. Combine steak, gherkins and marinade in bowl, cover, refrigerate several hours or overnight.

Drain steak and gherkins, reserve marinade. Thread steak and gherkins onto 8 skewers, grill or barbecue kebabs until steak is done as desired.

Meanwhile, place reserved marinade in pan, stir in blended cornflour and water, stir over heat until mixture boils and thickens. Serve sauce over kebabs. Serve with vegetables, salad or rice, if desired.

Mustard Marinade: Combine all ingredients in bowl; mix well.

Serves 4.

- Recipe can be prepared a day ahead.
- Storage: Covered, in refrigerator.
- Freeze: Not suitable.
- Microwave: Sauce suitable.

BARBECUED BEEF SPARE RIBS

12 (about 1½kg) beef spare ribs

MARINADE
1 onion, chopped
⅓ cup brown sugar
½ cup Worcestershire sauce
2 cups tomato sauce
¼ cup white vinegar
½ cup water
¾ cup oil
1 bay leaf

Combine ribs and marinade in large dish, cover, refrigerate 3 hours or overnight.

Drain ribs, reserve marinade. Place reserved marinade in pan, bring to boil, simmer, uncovered, until slightly thickened. Grill or barbecue ribs until browned and tender. Pour sauce over ribs. Serve with salad, if desired.

Marinade: Combine all ingredients in large dish; mix well.

Serves 4.

- Recipe can be prepared a day ahead.
- Storage: Covered, in refrigerator.
- Freeze: Marinated ribs suitable.
- Microwave: Not suitable.

SAUCY DEVILLED MEATBALLS

500g minced beef
1 onion, chopped
2 cups (140g) stale breadcrumbs
1 egg, lightly beaten
1 small beef stock cube, crumbled
2 tablespoons tomato sauce
2 teaspoons Worcestershire sauce
2 tablespoons oil
2 x 410g cans tomatoes
½ cup water
1 small beef stock cube, crumbled, extra
1 tablespoon tomato sauce, extra
1 teaspoon Worcestershire sauce, extra
1 tablespoon chopped fresh basil
1 teaspoon sugar
375g spaghetti pasta

Process mince, onion, breadcrumbs, egg, stock cube and sauces until well combined. Shape mixture into about 20 balls, flatten slightly.

Heat oil in large pan, add meatballs, cook, stirring occasionally, until browned all over. Add undrained crushed tomatoes, water, extra stock cube, extra sauces, basil and sugar. Simmer, uncovered, about 5 minutes or until the meatballs are tender.

Meanwhile, add pasta to large pan of boiling water, boil, uncovered, until pasta is just tender; drain. Serve meatballs and sauce over pasta.

Serves 4.

■ Recipe can be made a day ahead.
■ Storage: Covered, in refrigerator.
■ Freeze: Meatballs and sauce suitable.
■ Microwave: Pasta suitable.

LEFT: Garlic Mustard Steak Salad.
ABOVE: Clockwise from left: Saucy Devilled Meatballs, Barbecued Beef Spare Ribs, Beef Kebabs with Mustard Marinade.

Left: Plate from Villa Italiana; napkin from Butler & Co. Above: Plates from Villa Italiana; garlic bowl from Mosmania; cloth from Accoutrement

❖❖ T-BONE STEAKS WITH MUSHROOM CITRUS SAUCE

4 T-bone steaks
2 tablespoons oil

MARINADE
1 cup (20g) dried Chinese
  mushrooms, sliced
1 tablespoon grated orange rind
1 cup orange juice
¼ cup hoi sin sauce
½ teaspoon ground cinnamon
1 teaspoon ground saffron
2 tablespoons white vinegar
½ cup dry white wine
3 green shallots, chopped

Combine steaks and marinade in bowl, cover, refrigerate 3 hours or overnight.

Remove steaks from marinade, reserve marinade. Heat reserved marinade in pan, bring to boil, simmer, uncovered, few minutes or until slightly thickened. Heat oil in large pan, cook steaks until done as desired; serve with sauce. Serve steaks with rice or salad, if desired.

Marinade: Combine all ingredients in bowl; mix well.

Serves 4.

- ■ Recipe can be prepared a day ahead.
- ■ Storage: Covered, in refrigerator.
- ■ Freeze: Not suitable.
- ■ Microwave: Not suitable.

CREAMY BEEF STROGANOFF

700g rump steak
plain flour
2 tablespoons oil
1 onion, chopped
3 teaspoons paprika
200g mushrooms, sliced
8 gherkins, sliced
2 cups milk
300g carton sour cream
2 teaspoons lemon juice
2 green shallots, chopped

Cut steak into thin strips. Toss steak in flour, shake away excess flour. Heat oil in large pan, add steak, cook, stirring, until lightly browned; remove steak from pan.

Add onion to same pan, cook, stirring, until soft, stir in paprika, mushrooms and gherkins, cook, stirring, 1 minute. Stir in milk, cream and juice, bring to boil, simmer, uncovered, about 8 minutes or until sauce is thickened. Return steak to pan, cook until heated through.

Sprinkle stroganoff with shallots. Serve with rice or noodles and salad, if desired.

Serves 4.

- ■ Recipe best made just before serving
- ■ Freeze: Not suitable.
- ■ Microwave: Not suitable.

SUPER BEEF BURGERS

500g minced beef
1 small beef stock cube, crumbled
1 onion, grated
1 teaspoon cracked black
  peppercorns
¼ cup stale breadcrumbs
oil for shallow-frying
2 onions, sliced, extra
4 hamburger rolls, halved
4 cheese slices
2 tomatoes, sliced
125g punnet alfalfa sprouts
2 (about 380g) fresh beetroot, finely
  chopped
½ bunch watercress

BARBECUE SAUCE
½ cup tomato sauce
1 small red pepper, finely chopped
1 tablespoon Worcestershire sauce
¼ teaspoon chilli powder

Combine beef, stock cube, grated onion, peppercorns and breadcrumbs in bowl. Divide mixture into 4, roll into balls, flatten slightly. Shallow-fry patties in hot oil with extra sliced onions until cooked; drain on absorbent paper. Toast rolls, fill with patties, onions, barbecue sauce, cheese, tomatoes, sprouts, beetroot and watercress.
Barbecue Sauce: Combine all ingredients in bowl; mix well.

Serves 4.
- Patties and barbecue sauce can be prepared separately a day ahead.
- Storage: Separately, covered, in refrigerator.
- Freeze: Uncooked patties suitable.
- Microwave: Not suitable.

LEFT: T-bone Steaks with Mushroom Citrus Sauce.
ABOVE: From left: Creamy Beef Stroganoff, Super Beef Burgers.

Left: Plate, napkin from Accoutrement
Above: Plates from Corso de Fiori

BEEF

STEAKS WITH MUSTARD PEPPERCORN SAUCE

50g butter
2 tablespoons olive oil
2 cloves garlic, crushed
4 sirloin steaks
1 tablespoon seeded mustard
2 teaspoons canned drained
    green peppercorns
1 cup dry white wine
1 tablespoon chopped fresh basil
40g butter, chopped, extra

Heat butter and oil in pan, add garlic and steaks, cook steaks until done as desired, remove steaks from pan.

Add mustard, peppercorns, wine and basil to pan, stir over heat 2 minutes, remove pan from heat, quickly whisk in extra butter. Serve steaks with mustard peppercorn sauce. Serve with vegetables or salad, if desired.

Serves 4.

- Recipe best made just before serving.
- Freeze: Not suitable.
- Microwave: Not suitable.

SPICY RED CABBAGE AND BEEF SALAD

8 slices (about 320g) rare roast beef
1/4 small (about 350g) red cabbage,
    shredded
4 green shallots, chopped
1 yellow pepper, chopped
2 tablespoons drained capers
2 tablespoons chopped fresh parsley
1/2 teaspoon dried marjoram leaves
1/3 cup olive oil
1/4 cup white wine vinegar
1 clove garlic, crushed
2 teaspoons horseradish cream

Slice beef into strips. Combine all ingredients in bowl, mix gently.

Serves 4.

- Recipe can be made 3 hours ahead.
- Storage: Covered, in refrigerator.
- Freeze: Not suitable.
- Microwave: Not suitable

CHILLI AND HONEY STEAKS

4 New York-style steaks

MARINADE
1/3 cup lime juice
1/4 cup olive oil
2 teaspoons dried oregano leaves
2 tablespoons honey
1 teaspoon dried chilli flakes
2 cloves garlic, crushed

Combine steaks and marinade in bowl, cover, refrigerate 3 hours or overnight.

Remove steaks from marinade, discard marinade. Barbecue, grill or pan-fry steaks until done as desired. Serve with pasta and vegetables, if desired.
Marinade: Combine all ingredients in bowl; mix well.

Serves 4.
- Recipe can be prepared a day ahead.
- Storage: Covered, in refrigerator.
- Freeze: Not suitable.
- Microwave: Not suitable.

STEAKS WITH OLIVES AND SUN-DRIED TOMATOES

4 Scotch fillet steaks
1 teaspoon cracked black
    peppercorns
1 tablespoon oil
1 red Spanish onion, sliced
3 cloves garlic, crushed
1/3 cup brandy
410g can tomatoes
1/2 cup sun-dried tomatoes,
    drained, sliced
1/3 cup black olives, halved
1 teaspoon castor sugar
2 tablespoons chopped fresh basil

Flatten steaks between sheets of plastic wrap with meat mallet until 2cm thick. Rub pepper into both sides of steak.

Heat oil in pan, add steaks, cook until done as desired, remove steaks from pan.

Add onion and garlic to pan, cook, stirring, until onion is soft. Add brandy to pan, carefully ignite, allow flames to subside. Stir in undrained crushed tomatoes, sun-dried tomatoes, olives, sugar and basil. Bring to boil, simmer, uncovered, 2 minutes. Serve sauce over steaks. Serve with vegetables or salad, if desired.

Serves 4.

- Recipe best made just before serving.
- Freeze: Not suitable.
- Microwave: Not suitable.

LEFT: Clockwise from left: Spicy Red Cabbage and Beef Salad, Chilli and Honey Steaks, Steaks with Mustard Peppercorn Sauce.
BELOW: Steaks with Olives and Sun-Dried Tomatoes.

Below: Plates from The Bay Tree; tiles from Country Floors. Left: China from Villeroy & Boch; tiles from Country Floors

STEAKS WITH MUSTARD CREAM SAUCE

2 teaspoons oil
4 beef eye-fillet steaks
1 teaspoon oil, extra
2 bacon rashers, chopped
2 green shallots, sliced
1 teaspoon French mustard
1 tablespoon brandy
½ cup thickened cream
1 tablespoon chopped fresh parsley
½ teaspoon cracked black
  peppercorns

Heat oil in large pan, add steaks, cook until done as desired; remove from pan.

Add extra oil, bacon and shallots to pan, cook, stirring, until bacon is crisp. Stir in mustard, brandy, cream, parsley and peppercorns, stir until mixture boils. Serve sauce over steak. Serve with vegetables or salad, if desired.

Serves 4.

■ Recipe best made just before serving.
■ Freeze: Not suitable.
■ Microwave: Not suitable.

SESAME BEEF SALAD WITH SNOW PEAS

1 tablespoon oil
500g piece rump steak
1 bunch (12 spears) asparagus,
  halved
250g snow peas
1 red pepper, chopped
6 green shallots, chopped
100g baby mushrooms, sliced
425g can baby corn, drained

DRESSING
¼ cup oil
2 tablespoons rice vinegar
1 tablespoon light soy sauce
2 teaspoons sesame oil
½ teaspoon sambal oelek

Heat oil in pan, add steak, cook until done as desired. Cut steak into thin slices.

Boil, steam or microwave asparagus and peas separately until just tender; rinse under cold water, drain. Combine steak, asparagus, peas, pepper, shallots, mushrooms and corn in bowl, add dressing; toss gently.

Dressing: Combine all ingredients in jar; shake well.

Serves 4.

■ Salad can be prepared 3 hours ahead.
■ Storage: Covered, in refrigerator.
■ Freeze: Not suitable.
■ Microwave: Vegetables suitable.

BELOW: From top: Steaks with Mustard Cream Sauce, Sesame Beef Salad with Snow Peas.

China from Villeroy & Boch; cloth from Home and Garden; jug from Mosmania

SPICY BEEF AND CORN TACOS

2 tablespoons oil
1 red Spanish onion, chopped
1 green pepper, chopped
1 teaspoon chilli powder
1 teaspoon ground cumin
500g minced beef
½ cup drained corn kernels
1 tablespoon tomato paste
1 tablespoon chopped
fresh coriander
8 taco shells
¼ bunch (about 10 leaves) English
spinach, shredded
1 tomato, chopped
½ cup sour cream
1 cup (125g) grated tasty cheese

Heat oil in pan, add onion, pepper and spices, cook, stirring, until onion is soft. Add mince, cook, stirring, until well browned. Stir in corn, paste and coriander.

Spoon mince mixture into heated taco shells. Top with spinach, tomato, sour cream and cheese.

Serves 4.

- Mince mixture can be made a day ahead.
- Storage: Covered, in refrigerator.
- Freeze: Mince mixture suitable.
- Microwave: Not suitable.

◆ HOT SAUSAGE
◆ AND STEAK KEBABS

3 (about 300g) hot Italian sausages
250g rump steak
1 small green pepper
1 red Spanish onion
12 (about 120g) baby mushrooms
12 (about 250g) cherry tomatoes
2 tablespoons oil
1 tablespoon tomato sauce
curly endive

MARINADE
2 teaspoons seeded mustard
1 tablespoon brown sugar
¼ cup light soy sauce
2 teaspoons olive oil
¼ cup dry sherry

Cut each sausage into 4 pieces. Cut steak into 3cm cubes and pepper into 3cm pieces. Cut onion into 12 pieces.

Thread some sausage pieces, steak, pepper, onion, a mushroom and a tomato onto 12 skewers. Pour marinade over kebabs in dish, cover, refrigerate several hours or overnight.

Remove kebabs from marinade, reserve marinade. Heat oil in pan, cook kebabs in batches until meat is tender, remove from pan. Stir sauce and reserved marinade into pan, bring to boil. Serve kebabs on endive topped with sauce.

Marinade: Combine all ingredients in bowl; mix well.

Serves 4.

- Recipe can be prepared a day ahead.
- Storage: Covered, in refrigerator.
- Freeze: Not suitable.
- Microwave: Not suitable.

ABOVE: From left: Spicy Beef and Corn Tacos, Hot Sausage and Steak Kebabs.

Plates from Home and Garden; tiles from Country Floors; napkin from Butler & Co.; basket from Mosmania

RISSOLES WITH TOMATO SAUCE

750g minced beef
1 cup (70g) stale breadcrumbs
⅓ cup grated parmesan cheese
1 clove garlic, crushed
2 tablespoons chopped fresh parsley
2 tablespoons chopped fresh basil
2 eggs, lightly beaten
plain flour
2 tablespoons oil

TOMATO SAUCE
300g can Tomato Supreme
1 small red pepper, sliced
1 tablespoon chopped fresh basil

Combine mince, breadcrumbs, cheese, garlic, herbs and eggs in large bowl, mix well. Divide mixture into 12 portions, shape into rissoles. Toss rissoles in flour, shake away excess flour.

Heat oil in pan, cook rissoles until browned and cooked through. Serve with tomato sauce. Serve with pasta, rice or vegetables, if desired.

Tomato Sauce: Combine all ingredients in pan, stir over heat until boiling.

Serves 4.

■ Recipe can be made a day ahead.
■ Storage: Covered, in refrigerator.
■ Freeze: Rissoles suitable.
■ Microwave: Sauce suitable.

TERIYAKI BEEF STIR-FRY

600g piece rump steak
2 tablespoons oil
1 tablespoon sesame oil
2 cloves garlic, sliced
4 green shallots, chopped
1 red pepper, sliced
½ cup bean sprouts
230g can bamboo shoots, drained
⅓ cup roasted unsalted cashews
½ cup honey
¼ cup teriyaki sauce
1 teaspoon garam masala
1 tablespoon tomato paste
1 small beef stock cube, crumbled
2 teaspoons cornflour
⅓ cup water

Cut steak into thin strips. Heat oils in large pan or wok, add garlic and steak, stir-fry until steak is browned. Add shallots, pepper, sprouts, bamboo shoots and nuts, stir-fry 2 minutes. Stir in honey, sauce, garam masala, paste, stock cube and blended cornflour and water. Stir-fry until mixture boils and thickens. Serve with rice, if desired.

Serves 4.

- ■ Recipe best made just before serving.
- ■ Freeze: Not suitable.
- ■ Microwave: Not suitable.

◆ STEAK WITH HERB VINAIGRETTE

500g piece round steak
1 clove garlic, crushed
2 tablespoons olive oil
½ cup dry red wine
1 tablespoon oil
2 pitta pocket breads
2 medium (about 260g) tomatoes, sliced

HERB VINAIGRETTE
¼ cup chopped fresh parsley
2 teaspoons dried rosemary leaves
⅓ cup olive oil
1 tablespoon white wine vinegar
¼ teaspoon sugar
1 small red Spanish onion, chopped

Combine steak, garlic, olive oil and wine in bowl, cover, refrigerate several hours or overnight.

Drain steak from marinade, discard marinade. Heat oil in pan, add steak, cook until done as desired; cut into strips. Split breads open, top with tomato, steak and herb vinaigrette. Serve with salad, if desired.
Herb Vinaigrette: Combine all ingredients in bowl; mix well.

Serves 4.

- ■ Recipe can be prepared a day ahead.
- ■ Storage: Covered, in refrigerator.
- ■ Freeze: Marinated steak suitable.
- ■ Microwave: Not suitable.

BEEF AND SPRING ONIONS IN RED WINE SAUCE

1 tablespoon oil
4 beef eye-fillet steaks
30g butter
8 spring onions
2 cloves garlic, crushed
1 cup dry red wine
½ cup water
1 small beef stock cube, crumbled
200g mushrooms, sliced
2 teaspoons cornflour
2 teaspoons water, extra

Heat oil in large pan, add steaks, cook until done as desired, remove steaks from pan. Add butter and onions to pan, cook, stirring, until onions are lightly browned. Stir in garlic, wine, water and stock cube, bring to boil, simmer, covered, 10 minutes.

Add mushrooms, cook, stirring, until

mushrooms are tender, stir in blended cornflour and extra water, stir over heat until sauce boils and thickens. Serve steaks with sauce. Serve with vegetables, if desired.

Serves 4.

- ■ Recipe best made just before serving.
- ■ Freeze: Not suitable.
- ■ Microwave: Not suitable.

BEEF PATTIES WITH CHEESY POTATO TOPPING

500g minced beef
¼ cup packaged breadcrumbs
2 cloves garlic, crushed
1 tablespoon Worcestershire sauce
¼ cup chopped fresh parsley
1 tablespoon lemon juice
1 teaspoon cracked black peppercorns
1 egg yolk
2 tablespoons oil
¼ cup grated tasty cheese
1 tablespoon chopped fresh chives

POTATO TOPPING
1 large (about 200g) potato, chopped
1 tablespoon milk
30g butter
1 tablespoon chopped fresh chives
¼ cup grated tasty cheese

Combine mince, breadcrumbs, garlic,

sauce, parsley, juice, peppercorns and egg yolk in bowl; mix well. Shape mixture into 4 patties.

Heat oil in pan, add patties, cook until browned and cooked through. Spoon potato mixture onto patties, press gently, sprinkle with cheese. Grill patties until cheese is melted and lightly browned. Serve sprinkled with chives. Serve with salad, if desired.
Potato Topping: Boil, steam or microwave potato until tender, drain. Mash potato with milk and butter in bowl until smooth. Stir in chives and cheese.

Serves 4.

- ■ Patties can be prepared a day ahead.
- ■ Storage: Covered, in refrigerator.
- ■ Freeze: Uncooked patties, without potato, suitable.
- ■ Microwave: Potato suitable.

LEFT: Clockwise from top left: Rissoles with Tomato Sauce, Teriyaki Beef Stir-Fry, Steak with Herb Vinaigrette.
ABOVE: From back: Beef and Spring Onions in Red Wine Sauce, Beef Patties with Cheesy Potato Topping.

Left: China from Mikasa; fabric from Redelman Fabrics. Above: China from Wedgwood Waterford; fabric from Redelman Fabrics

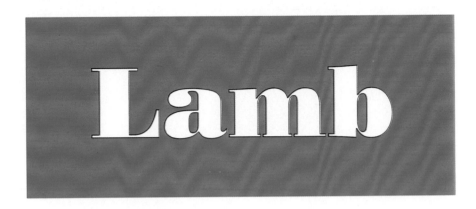

Lamb

■ *For speed, we've used only smaller pre-cut pieces such as steaks, chops and fillets, etc.* ■ *Most cuts are interchangeable, so use your favourites if you prefer.* ■ *For healthier eating, trim as much fat as possible before you cook.* ■ *Quickly seal in juices over high heat, then reduce heat to cook lamb as desired. Don't overcook or lamb will toughen.* ■ *Uncooked cuts slice easily if partly frozen; thaw completely before cooking.* ■ *Lamb cuts can be pre-cooked, cooled and frozen ready for use in many recipes.* ■ *Marinated recipes are indicated by this symbol* ❖ *this means you have to start ahead of time.*

❖ COCONUT LAMB CHOPS WITH ASPARAGUS SAUCE

8 lamb leg chops

MARINADE
¾ cup milk
1¼ cups coconut milk
1½ teaspoons sambal oelek
1½ tablespoons chopped fresh lemon grass
1½ tablespoons brown sugar
3 cloves garlic, crushed
¼ cup chopped roasted unsalted peanuts

ASPARAGUS SAUCE
30g butter
1 medium bunch (12 spears) fresh asparagus, chopped
6 green shallots, chopped
1 tablespoon plain flour
¼ cup water

Combine chops and ⅔ cup of the marinade in bowl, cover, refrigerate several hours or overnight. Reserve remaining marinade for sauce.

Drain chops from marinade, discard this marinade. Grill chops until tender. Serve with asparagus sauce. Serve with noodles or rice, if desired.
Marinade: Blend or process all ingredients until smooth.

Asparagus Sauce: Heat butter in pan, add asparagus and shallots, cook, stirring, until asparagus is just tender. Stir in flour, cook until mixture is dry and grainy. Remove from heat, gradually stir in reserved marinade and water. Stir over heat until mixture boils and thickens.

Serves 4.

■ Lamb can be prepared a day ahead.
■ Storage: Covered, in refrigerator.
■ Freeze: Marinated lamb suitable.
■ Microwave: Not suitable.

LAMB SAUTE WITH PEPPERS AND BASIL

4 lamb leg steaks
⅓ cup plain flour
1 teaspoon cracked black peppercorns
2 tablespoons olive oil
1 tablespoon olive oil, extra
1 yellow pepper, sliced
1 red pepper, sliced
8 green shallots, sliced
4 cloves garlic, crushed
¼ cup brandy
1 small beef stock cube, crumbled
¾ cup water
½ cup fresh basil leaves, shredded

Cut lamb into 3cm cubes. Toss lamb in combined flour and peppercorns, shake away excess flour. Heat oil in pan, add lamb, stir over heat until well browned and tender; remove lamb from pan.

Add extra oil to pan, stir in peppers, shallots and garlic, cook, stirring, 1 minute. Add brandy to pan, carefully ignite, allow flames to subside. Stir in combined stock cube and water, bring to boil, simmer, covered, 10 minutes. Stir in lamb and basil; stir until heated through. Serve with rice or pasta and vegetables, if desired.

Serves 4.

■ Recipe can be made a day ahead.
■ Storage: Covered, in refrigerator.
■ Freeze: Suitable.
■ Microwave: Not suitable.

RIGHT: From top: Lamb Saute with Peppers and Basil, Coconut Lamb Chops with Asparagus Sauce.

Plates from Mosmania

LAMB WITH PLUM GLAZE

The colouring in this recipe is not used for flavour; it can be left out, if preferred.

1 cup Chinese plum sauce
1 tablespoon light soy sauce
2 cloves garlic, crushed
1 tablespoon dry sherry
red food colouring
4 lamb leg chops

Combine sauces, garlic and sherry in bowl, stir in colouring, add lamb; mix well.

Place lamb on rack in baking dish, spoon over any remaining sauce mixture. Bake, uncovered, in hot oven about 15 minutes or until lamb is tender. Serve with salad, rice or noodles, if desired.

Serves 4.

■ Recipe best made just before serving.
■ Freeze: Uncooked lamb suitable.
■ Microwave: Not suitable.

WARM LAMB SALAD WITH SUN-DRIED TOMATOES

1 tablespoon olive oil
500g lamb fillets
1 clove garlic, crushed
¼ cup balsamic vinegar
¼ cup olive oil, extra
⅓ cup drained sun-dried tomatoes, sliced
15g butter
1 medium bunch (12 spears) fresh asparagus, chopped
1 red pepper, chopped
150g baby mushrooms, quartered
lettuce

Heat oil in pan, add lamb, cook until well browned and tender; slice lamb. Combine lamb, garlic, vinegar, extra oil and tomatoes in bowl.

Heat butter in same pan, add asparagus, pepper and mushrooms, cook, stirring, until asparagus is tender; add to lamb mixture in bowl, toss gently. Serve lamb mixture on lettuce leaves.

Serves 4.

■ Recipe best made just before serving.
■ Freeze: Not suitable.
■ Microwave: Not suitable.

❖ LAMBS' FRY WITH WHITE ❖ WINE SAUCE

650g lambs' fry
plain flour
2 tablespoons oil
1 onion, chopped
3 bacon rashers, sliced
2 teaspoons dried tarragon leaves
½ cup dry white wine
2 teaspoons white vinegar
300ml carton thickened cream
2 teaspoons cornflour
¼ cup water

Place lambs' fry in bowl, add enough cold water to cover fry. Cover bowl, refrigerate several hours or overnight.

Drain fry well, peel skin, cut fry into thin slices. Toss fry in flour, shake away excess flour. Heat oil in pan, add fry, cook until browned and just tender, remove fry from pan.

Add onion and bacon to pan, cook, stirring, until onion is soft. Stir in tarragon, wine, vinegar, cream and blended cornflour and water, stir until mixture boils and thickens. Serve over fry. Serve with vegetables, if desired.

Serves 4.

■ Lambs' fry can be prepared a day ahead.
■ Storage: Covered, in refrigerator.
■ Freeze: Not suitable.
■ Microwave: Not suitable.

LEFT: Clockwise from top left: Warm Lamb Salad with Sun-Dried Tomatoes, Lambs' Fry with White Wine Sauce, Lamb with Plum Glaze

Blue and white plates from Corso de Fiori

SPICY CORIANDER LAMB WITH APRICOTS

1 tablespoon oil
750g lamb fillets
1 onion, sliced
1 clove garlic, crushed
1 teaspoon ground cumin
1 teaspoon garam masala
2 small beef stock cubes, crumbled
825g can apricot halves
   in natural juice
1 teaspoon cornflour
1 teaspoon water
1 tablespoon chopped fresh coriander

Heat oil in pan, add lamb, cook until well browned and tender; remove lamb from pan, cut into slices. Add onion and garlic to same pan, cook, stirring, until onion is soft. Add spices, stock cubes and un-drained apricots, bring to boil, simmer, un-covered, 5 minutes. Stir in blended cornflour and water, stir until mixture boils and thickens. Add lamb, stir until heated through. Serve sprinkled with coriander. Serve with rice or pasta, if desired.

Serves 4.

■ Recipe can be made a day ahead.
■ Storage: Covered, in refrigerator.
■ Freeze: Suitable.
■ Microwave: Suitable.

ORANGE GINGER LAMB CHOPS

1 tablespoon oil
8 lamb chump chops
1 tablespoon oil, extra
1 onion, chopped
1 clove garlic, crushed
1 tablespoon grated fresh ginger
½ cup orange juice
¼ cup water
2 tablespoons light soy sauce
1 tablespoon honey
2 teaspoons castor sugar
2 teaspoons cornflour
2 teaspoons water, extra

Heat oil in large pan, add lamb, cook until browned and tender.

Meanwhile, heat extra oil in separate pan, add onion and garlic, cook, stirring, until onion is soft. Press ginger between 2 spoons to extract juice, discard pulp.

Add ginger juice, orange juice, water, sauce, honey, sugar and blended cornflour and extra water to pan; stir over heat until mixture boils and thickens. Serve sauce over chops. Serve with vegetables or salad, if desired.

Serves 4.

■ Sauce can be made a day ahead.
■ Storage: Covered, in refrigerator.
■ Freeze: Not suitable.
■ Microwave: Suitable.

NOISETTES OF LAMB WITH MUSTARD WINE SAUCE

1 tablespoon oil
8 lamb noisettes
2 tablespoons plain flour
1½ cups water
2 small beef stock cubes, crumbled
2 tablespoons tomato paste
2 tablespoon dry red wine
2 teaspoons seeded mustard
2 teaspoons Worcestershire sauce
1 teaspoon sugar

Heat oil in pan, add lamb, cook until tender, remove lamb from pan. Stir in flour, cook until grainy and browned. Remove from heat, stir in combined remaining in-gredients, stir over heat until mixture boils and thickens. Serve mustard wine sauce over lamb. Serve with pasta or vegetables, if desired.

Serves 4.

■ Recipe best made just before serving.
■ Freeze: Not suitable.
■ Microwave: Suitable.

GARLIC LAMB WITH MUSTARD HORSERADISH CREAM

2 cloves garlic, crushed
4 lamb leg steaks

MUSTARD HORSERADISH CREAM
¾ cup sour cream
3 teaspoons horseradish cream
1½ tablespoons chopped fresh mint
1 tablespoon seeded mustard

Rub garlic over lamb, grill or barbecue until browned and tender. Serve steaks with mustard horseradish cream. Serve with salad or vegetables, if desired.
Mustard Horseradish Cream: Combine all ingredients in bowl; mix well.

Serves 4.

■ Mustard horseradish cream can be prepared a day ahead.
■ Storage: Covered, in refrigerator.
■ Freeze: Not suitable.
■ Microwave: Not suitable.

LEFT: Spicy Coriander Lamb with Apricots.
RIGHT: Clockwise from top left: Noisettes of Lamb with Mustard Wine Sauce, Garlic Lamb with Mustard Horseradish Cream, Orange Ginger Lamb Chops.

Left: China from Johnson Bros/Wedgwood
Right: Plates from Amy's Tableware

MINI LAMB AND VEGETABLE PIES

1 tablespoon oil
1 onion, sliced
2 cloves garlic, crushed
750g minced lamb
1 cup (150g) frozen mixed vegetables
2 small beef stock cubes, crumbled
1 teaspoon dried rosemary leaves
¼ cup tomato paste
2 tablespoons barbecue sauce
1 cup water
½ cup dry white wine
1½ tablespoons plain flour
2 tablespoons water, extra
1 sheet ready-rolled puff pastry
1 tablespoon milk

Heat oil in pan, add onion and garlic, cook, stirring, until onion is soft. Add lamb, cook, stirring, until lamb is well browned all over. Add vegetables, stock cubes, rosemary, paste, sauce, water and wine; bring to boil, simmer, uncovered, 2 minutes. Stir in blended flour and extra water, stir until mixture boils and thickens. Spoon mixture into 4 ovenproof dishes (1 cup capacity).

Cut 4 circles from pastry large enough to cover dishes, place pastry on top of dishes. Brush pastry with milk, place dishes on oven tray. Bake in very hot oven about 5 minutes or until tops are puffed and well browned.

Serves 4.

■ Filling can be made a day ahead.
■ Storage: Covered, in refrigerator.
■ Freeze: Filling suitable.
■ Microwave: Not suitable.

RIGHT: Lamb Cutlets with Nutty Herb Butter.
BELOW: Clockwise from left: Lamb Coriander Salad, Mini Lamb and Vegetable Pies, Crunchy Lamb Fillets with Mango Sauce.

Below: China from Wedgwood; cloth from Redelman Fabrics. Right: China from Villeroy & Boch; napkin from Home and Garden

❖ LAMB CORIANDER SALAD

2 tablespoons oil
750g lamb fillets
2 medium (about 240g) carrots
curly endive
¼ cup chopped roasted
 unsalted cashews

MARINADE
⅓ cup chopped fresh coriander
⅓ cup lemon juice
2 tablespoons fish sauce
1 teaspoon sambal oelek
1 tablespoon crunchy peanut butter

Heat oil in pan, add lamb, cook until browned and tender, slice lamb. Combine lamb and marinade in bowl; cover, refrigerate several hours or overnight.

Peel thin ribbons from carrots using vegetable peeler. Place lamb mixture and carrot ribbons on endive leaves, sprinkle with nuts.
Marinade: Combine all ingredients in bowl; mix well.

Serves 4.

- Recipe can be prepared a day ahead.
- Storage: Covered, in refrigerator.
- Freeze: Not suitable.
- Microwave: Not suitable.

CRUNCHY LAMB FILLETS WITH MANGO SAUCE

2 cups (140g) stale breadcrumbs
¾ cup packaged ground almonds
2 tablespoons chopped fresh chives
2 tablespoons chopped fresh parsley
4 lamb fillets
plain flour
1 egg, lightly beaten
¼ cup milk
oil for shallow-frying

MANGO SAUCE
425g can mangoes in syrup
1 small chicken stock cube, crumbled
2 tablespoons cream
2 tablespoons water

Combine breadcrumbs, nuts and herbs in shallow dish. Toss lamb in flour, shake away excess flour, dip into combined egg and milk, toss in crumb mixture, press on firmly. Freeze 10 minutes.

Shallow-fry lamb in hot oil until lightly browned and tender. Serve lamb sliced with mango sauce. Serve with vegetables or salad, if desired.
Mango Sauce: Drain mangoes, reserve 2 tablespoons of syrup. Blend or process mangoes until smooth. Combine mango puree, reserved syrup, stock cube, cream and water in pan. Stir over heat until heated through.

Serves 4.

- Recipe can be prepared a day ahead.
- Storage: Covered, in refrigerator.
- Freeze: Uncooked crumbed lamb suitable.
- Microwave: Sauce suitable.

LAMB CUTLETS WITH NUTTY HERB BUTTER

1 tablespoon oil
8 lamb cutlets

NUTTY HERB BUTTER
125g butter, softened
2 green shallots, chopped
1 clove garlic, crushed
1 teaspoon dried thyme leaves
1 teaspoon dried sage leaves
¼ cup chopped roasted hazelnuts

Heat oil in pan, add lamb, cook until tender. Serve with nutty herb butter. Serve with vegetables or salad, if desired.

Nutty Herb Butter: Combine all ingredients in bowl; mix well.

Serves 4.

- Butter can be prepared a week ahead.
- Storage: Covered, in refrigerator.
- Freeze: Butter suitable.
- Microwave: Suitable.

LAMB WITH PEANUT CURRY SAUCE

4 lamb leg chops, chopped
1 tablespoon oil
30g butter
1 onion, sliced
3 cloves garlic, crushed
1 tablespoon light soy sauce
1 cup water
1 tablespoon vindaloo curry paste
½ cup smooth peanut butter

Heat oil in pan, add lamb in batches, cook, stirring, until well browned and tender.

Meanwhile, heat butter in pan, add onion, cook, stirring, until soft. Add remaining ingredients, stir over heat until sauce is thickened. Add lamb, stir until hot. Serve with rice, if desired.

Serves 4.

■ Recipe can be made a day ahead.
■ Storage: Covered, in refrigerator.
■ Freeze: Not suitable.
■ Microwave: Not suitable.

❖ BARBECUED CHILLI AND HONEY LAMB

8 lamb cutlets

MARINADE
2 cloves garlic, crushed
1 tablespoon seeded mustard
1 teaspoon grated lemon rind
2 tablespoons lemon juice
2 tablespoons honey
2 teaspoons curry powder
1 teaspoon sambal oelek
1 teaspoon turmeric

Rub marinade into lamb; place in bowl, cover, refrigerate 3 hours or overnight.

Barbecue or grill lamb until tender. Serve with vegetables or salad, if desired.
Marinade: Combine all ingredients in bowl; mix well.

Serves 4.

■ Recipe can be prepared a day ahead.
■ Storage: Covered, in refrigerator.
■ Freeze: Marinated lamb suitable.
■ Microwave: Not suitable.

◆◆ LAMB IN FRUITY CHUTNEY MARINADE

4 lamb shoulder chops

MARINADE
½ cup chutney
2 tablespoons oil
2 teaspoons French mustard
½ teaspoon cracked black
peppercorns

Combine chops and marinade in bowl, cover, refrigerate 3 hours or overnight.
Barbecue or grill chops until tender. Serve with salad or vegetables, if desired.
Marinade: Combine all ingredients in bowl; mix well.

Serves 4.

■ Recipe can be prepared a day ahead.
■ Storage: Covered, in refrigerator.
■ Freeze: Marinated chops suitable.
■ Microwave: Not suitable.

LAMB KEBABS WITH APRICOT SAUCE

6 lamb leg chops
2 tablespoons oil
1 teaspoon dried rosemary leaves
1 teaspoon cracked black
peppercorns
16 pimiento-stuffed green olives
1 tablespoon oil, extra

APRICOT SAUCE
1 cup apricot nectar
¼ cup dry white wine
3 teaspoons cornflour
1 tablespoon water
1 tablespoon chopped fresh mint

Cut lamb into 2cm pieces. Combine lamb, oil, rosemary and pepper in bowl. Thread lamb onto 8 skewers. Thread olives onto ends of skewers.
Heat extra oil in pan, add kebabs, cook until well browned and tender. Serve with apricot sauce. Serve with rice, if desired.

Apricot Sauce: Combine nectar, wine and blended cornflour and water in pan, stir over heat until mixture boils and thickens; stir in mint.

Serves 4.

■ Kebabs and sauce can be prepared a day ahead.
■ Storage: Covered, in refrigerator.
■ Freeze: Uncooked kebabs suitable.
■ Microwave: Sauce suitable.

LEFT: From top: Lamb with Peanut Curry Sauce, Barbecued Chilli and Honey Lamb.
ABOVE: From top: Lamb in Fruity Chutney Marinade, Lamb Kebabs with Apricot Sauce.

Left: Cloth from Mosmania. Above: China from Mikasa; tiles from Country Floors

MINTED LAMB KOFTA WITH CUCUMBER SAUCE

500g minced lamb
3 green shallots, chopped
½ cup stale breadcrumbs
2 teaspoons chopped fresh mint
2 tablespoons lemon juice
½ teaspoon ground cumin
1 egg, lightly beaten
plain flour
2 tablespoons oil

CUCUMBER SAUCE
⅓ cup plain yogurt
¼ teaspoon ground cinnamon
¼ teaspoon ground cumin
¼ teaspoon ground coriander
1 small green cucumber, grated

Combine lamb, shallots, breadcrumbs, mint, juice, cumin and egg in bowl, mix well. Shape level tablespoons of mixture into balls, toss in flour, shake away excess flour. Heat oil in pan, add meatballs, cook until tender; drain on absorbent paper. Serve with cucumber sauce. Serve with vegetables or salad, if desired.
Cucumber Sauce: Combine all ingredients in bowl; mix well.

Serves 4.

■ Recipe can be made a day ahead.
■ Storage: Covered, in refrigerator.
■ Freeze: Meatballs suitable.
■ Microwave: Not suitable.

LAMB CUTLETS WITH SWEET CITRUS SAUCE

2 tablespoons oil
8 lamb cutlets

SWEET CITRUS SAUCE
1 tablespoon shredded orange rind
⅓ cup orange juice
2 tablespoons lemon juice
½ cup redcurrant jelly
1 tablespoon red wine vinegar
½ teaspoon cracked black peppercorns
4 green shallots, chopped
2 teaspoons cornflour
1 tablespoon water

Heat oil in pan, cook lamb until tender. Serve lamb with sweet citrus sauce. Serve with vegetables or salad, if desired.

Sweet Citrus Sauce: Combine rind, juices, jelly, vinegar, pepper and shallots in pan, stir over heat until jelly is melted and shallots are soft. Stir in blended cornflour and water, stir over heat   until sauce boils and thickens.

Serves 4.

■ Sauce can be made a day ahead.
■ Storage: Covered, in refrigerator.
■ Freeze: Not suitable.
■ Microwave: Sauce suitable.

LAMB WITH GOATS' CHEESE AND OLIVES

2 tablespoons oil
4 lamb noisettes
3 bacon rashers, sliced
1/3 cup drained sun-dried tomatoes, sliced
1/3 cup pimiento-stuffed green olives, halved
2 teaspoons dried rosemary leaves
1/4 cup lime juice
1/2 cup water
70g butter, chopped
1/2 cup fresh basil leaves, shredded
150g goats' cheese, chopped

Heat oil in pan, add lamb, cook until browned and tender, remove from pan.

Pour excess oil from pan, add bacon, cook, stirring, until crisp, add tomatoes, olives, rosemary, juice and water. Bring to boil, remove pan from heat, quickly whisk in butter, stir in basil and cheese. Serve lamb with sauce. Serve with grilled zucchini, baby eggplant and pimientos or salad, if desired.

Serves 4.

■ Recipe best made just before serving.
■ Freeze: Not suitable.
■ Microwave: Not suitable.

LEFT: From left: Minted Lamb Kofta with Cucumber Sauce, Lamb Cutlets with Sweet Citrus Sauce.
ABOVE: Lamb with Goats' Cheese and Olives.

Above: China from Villeroy & Boch; white Pillivuyt jug from Hale Imports; basket from Mosmania; napkin from Home and Garden; tiles from Pazotti
Left: Jug from Accoutrement; mats from Butler & Co

LAMB WITH PESTO AND PARMESAN TOMATOES

8 lamb loin chops

PESTO
**½ cup fresh basil leaves,
   firmly packed
2 teaspoons chopped fresh mint
4 cloves garlic, crushed
½ cup olive oil
¼ cup grated parmesan cheese**

PARMESAN TOMATOES
**2 large (about 500g) tomatoes, halved
30g butter, melted
2 cloves garlic, crushed
1 cup (70g) stale breadcrumbs
⅓ cup grated parmesan cheese
2 tablespoons chopped fresh basil**

Brush both sides of lamb with pesto, reserve remaining pesto. Grill lamb until browned and tender. Serve with reserved pesto and parmesan tomatoes. Serve with salad or vegetables, if desired.
Pesto: Blend or process all ingredients until well combined.
Parmesan Tomatoes: Grill tomato halves until heated through. Combine butter, garlic, crumbs, cheese and basil in bowl; mix well. Top tomato halves with cheese mixture, grill until lightly browned.

Serves 4.
- Pesto can be prepared a day ahead.
- Storage: Covered, in refrigerator
- Freeze: Not suitable.
- Microwave: Not suitable.

LAMB WITH EGGPLANTS AND PEPPERS

**2 tablespoons olive oil
8 lamb noisettes
8 small (about 250g) eggplants, sliced
1 red pepper, sliced
1 green pepper, sliced
1 yellow pepper, sliced**

Heat oil in pan, add lamb, cook until tender, remove lamb from pan. Add eggplants to pan, cook, stirring, until just tender, remove from pan. Add peppers to pan, cook, stirring, until soft. Serve lamb on eggplants, topped with peppers. Serve with salad, if desired.

Serves 4.
- Recipe best made just before serving.
- Freeze: Not suitable.
- Microwave: Not suitable.

❖ CURRIED LAMB STEAKS WITH YOGURT

**4 lamb leg steaks
250g carton plain yogurt
1 tablespoon chopped fresh coriander**

MARINADE
**2 tablespoons oil
1 tablespoon curry powder
1 teaspoon ground cumin
½ teaspoon turmeric
2 cloves garlic, crushed
1 onion, chopped
2 tablespoons mango chutney
2 tablespoons brown vinegar**

Combine lamb and marinade in bowl, cover, refrigerate 3 hours or overnight.
  Remove lamb from marinade, discard marinade. Grill lamb until browned and tender. Serve lamb with combined yogurt and coriander. Serve with rice or vegetables, if desired.
Marinade: Combine all ingredients in bowl; mix well.

Serves 4.
- Recipe can be prepared a day ahead.
- Storage: Covered, in refrigerator.
- Freeze: Marinated lamb suitable.
- Microwave: Not suitable.

❖ PITTA SALAD ROLLS WITH LAMB KEBABS

**6 lamb leg chops
2 tablespoons olive oil
lettuce, shredded
2 tomatoes, sliced
½ cup black olives, quartered
200g feta cheese, chopped
8 pitta pocket breads**

MARINADE
**¼ cup lemon juice
2 tablespoons olive oil
1 small chicken stock cube, crumbled
1 clove garlic, crushed**

Cut lamb into 2cm cubes. Combine lamb and marinade in bowl, cover, refrigerate several hours or overnight. Remove lamb from marinade, reserve marinade. Thread lamb onto 8 skewers. Heat reserved marinade and oil in pan, add kebabs, cook, turning, until lamb is tender.
  Place lettuce, tomatoes, olives and cheese on pitta breads, top with kebabs. Remove skewers and roll pitta breads around lamb.
Marinade: Combine all ingredients in bowl; mix well.

Serves 4.
- Recipe can be prepared a day ahead.
- Storage: Covered, in refrigerator.
- Freeze: Marinated lamb suitable.
- Microwave: Not suitable.

*LEFT: Clockwise from top left: Lamb with Pesto and Parmesan Tomatoes, Curried Lamb Steaks with Yogurt, Lamb with Eggplants and Peppers.
RIGHT: Pitta Salad Rolls with Lamb Kebabs.*

Plates from Villa Italiana; cutlery from Jarass. Right: Platter and napkin from Accoutrement

NUTTY LAMB CUTLETS WITH CHUTNEY SAUCE

⅓ cup packaged ground almonds
⅓ cup packaged ground hazelnuts
½ cup packaged breadcrumbs
8 lamb cutlets
plain flour
2 eggs, lightly beaten
¼ cup oil

CHUTNEY SAUCE
½ cup chutney
2 tablespoons water
2 tablespoons chopped fresh parsley

Combine nuts and breadcrumbs in bowl; mix well. Toss cutlets in flour; shake away excess flour, dip into eggs, toss in nut mixture, shake away excess mixture.

Heat oil in large pan, cook cutlets until well browned and tender. Serve cutlets with hot chutney sauce. Serve with vegetables or salad, if desired.
Chutney Sauce: Combine all ingredients in pan; heat without boiling.

Serves 4.

■ Recipe can be prepared a day ahead.
■ Storage: Covered, in refrigerator.
■ Freeze: Uncooked crumbed cutlets suitable.
■ Microwave: Sauce suitable.

LAMB AND SPINACH VOL-AU-VENTS

1 tablespoon oil
750g lamb leg steaks, sliced
1 red Spanish onion, chopped
150g mushrooms, chopped
½ bunch (20 leaves) English spinach, shredded
30g butter
2 tablespoons plain flour
1½ cups milk
¼ teaspoon ground nutmeg
½ cup grated tasty cheese
4 x 125mm (60g) vol-au-vent cases
125g feta cheese, crumbled
paprika

Heat oil in pan, add lamb and onion, cook, stirring, until lamb is tender. Add mushrooms and spinach, cook, stirring, until spinach is wilted. Remove lamb mixture from pan; drain.

Meanwhile, heat butter in separate pan, add flour, cook, stirring, until mixture is dry and grainy, remove from heat, gradually stir in milk, stir over heat until sauce boils and thickens. Remove pan from heat, stir in nutmeg, tasty cheese and lamb mixture.

Divide mixture between vol-au-vent cases, top with feta cheese, sprinkle with paprika. Place vol-au-vents onto oven trays, bake, uncovered, in moderately hot oven about 10 minutes or until hot. Serve with salad or vegetables, if desired.

Serves 4.

■ Recipe can be prepared several hours ahead.
■ Storage: Covered, in refrigerator.
■ Freeze: Not suitable.
■ Microwave: Sauce suitable.

BELOW: From left: Nutty Lamb Cutlets with Chutney Sauce Lamb and Spinach Vol-au-Vents
RIGHT: Lamb with Blueberry Mint Sauce.

LAMB WITH BLUEBERRY MINT SAUCE

425g can blueberries in syrup
15g butter
1 tablespoon oil
4 racks of lamb (4 cutlets each), boned
1 clove garlic, crushed
2 bacon rashers, chopped
½ cup water
2 teaspoons lemon juice
1 tablespoon chopped fresh mint
2 teaspoons cornflour
2 teaspoons water, extra

Drain blueberries, reserve half the blueberries and quarter cup of the syrup. Remaining blueberries and syrup are not used in this recipe.

Heat butter and oil in pan, add lamb, cook until browned and tender, remove lamb from pan. Discard all but 1 tablespoon of pan juices, add garlic and bacon to pan, cook, stirring, until bacon is crisp. Add reserved blueberry syrup, water, lemon juice and mint to pan. Bring to boil, simmer, uncovered, 2 minutes.

Stir in blended cornflour and extra water, stir over heat until mixture boils and thickens. Add reserved blueberries, stir over heat until heated through. Serve sauce over sliced lamb. Serve with vegetables, if desired.

Serves 4.

■ Recipe best made just before serving.
■ Freeze: Not suitable.
■ Microwave: Not suitable.

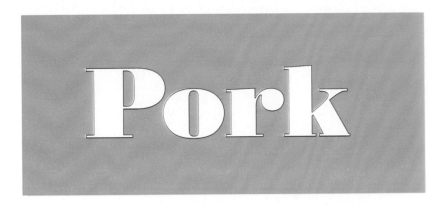

Pork

■ *Today's pork is leaner and dries out quickly, so be careful not to overcook it or it will toughen.* ■ *Cook on high heat briefly at first to seal the outside, then reduce heat to moderate until pork is cooked as specified.* ■ *The smaller cuts are ideal for speedy cooking and you can substitute any cut for another. We've also included ham, prosciutto and tasty salami-type sausages.* ■ *Leaner pork is suitable for healthy eating, with little fat to trim; however, it's always a good idea to trim any visible fat.* ■ *We like pork for stir-fries; it seems especially delicious.* ■ *Microwaved pork is good, so use a browning plate for top results.* ■ *Marinated recipes are indicated by this symbol* ❖ *this means you need to start ahead of time.*

HAM, KUMARA AND BEAN SALAD

500g kumara, chopped
200g green beans, sliced
3 ham steaks
410g can potatoes, drained, quartered
¼ cup chopped fresh chives

DRESSING
1 egg yolk
1 tablespoon white vinegar
½ cup olive oil
1 tablespoon orange juice

Boil, steam or microwave kumara and beans separately until just tender, drain. Cut ham into strips. Combine kumara, beans, ham, potatoes and chives in bowl. Pour dressing over salad.
Dressing: Blend or process egg yolk and vinegar until smooth. Add oil gradually in a thin stream while motor is operating, stir in orange juice.
Serves 4.

■ Recipe can be made a day ahead.
■ Storage: Covered, in refrigerator.
■ Freeze: Not suitable.
■ Microwave: Suitable.

PORK WITH PEAR AND GINGER SAUCE

4 pork butterfly steaks
½ cup plain flour
1 tablespoon seasoned pepper
2 tablespoons oil

PEAR AND GINGER SAUCE
250g dried pears, quartered
2 cups water
1 chicken stock cube, crumbled
2 tablespoons chopped glace ginger
1 tablespoon lemon juice

Toss pork in combined flour and pepper, shake away excess flour. Heat oil in pan, cook steaks on both sides until tender. Serve with pear and ginger sauce. Serve with vegetables or salad, if desired.

Pear and Ginger Sauce: Combine pears, water and stock cube in pan, bring to boil, boil, covered, about 5 minutes or until pears are soft. Blend or process pear mixture with ginger and juice until smooth.
Serves 4.

■ Pear and ginger sauce can be made a day ahead.
■ Storage: Covered, in refrigerator.
■ Freeze: Not suitable.
■ Microwave: Sauce suitable.

RIGHT: From top: Pork with Pear and Ginger Sauce, Ham, Kumara and Bean Salad.

Plate from Royal Doulton

PORK WITH WHITE WINE AND MUSHROOM SAUCE

20g butter
1 tablespoon oil
600g pork fillets
1 tablespoon oil, extra
1 onion, sliced
100g mushrooms, sliced
1 teaspoon dried thyme leaves
¾ cup dry white wine
½ cup water
1 small beef stock cube, crumbled
¼ cup cream
2 teaspoons cornflour
2 teaspoons water, extra

Heat butter and oil in pan, add pork, cook until well browned all over. Transfer pork to ovenproof dish, pour over pan juices. Bake, covered, in moderately hot oven about 20 minutes or until tender.

Meanwhile, heat extra oil in pan, add onion and mushrooms, cook, stirring, until onion is soft. Add thyme, wine, water and stock cube; bring to boil, simmer, uncovered, 5 minutes. Stir in cream and blended cornflour and extra water, stir over heat until sauce boils and thickens. Serve sauce over sliced pork. Serve with vegetables or rice, if desired.

Serves 4.

■ Recipe best made just before serving.
■ Freeze: Not suitable.
■ Microwave: Not suitable.

❖ PORK WITH ORANGE GINGER SAUCE

4 pork butterfly steaks
2 tablespoons oil

MARINADE
1 teaspoon grated orange rind
1 cup orange juice
2 tablespoons light soy sauce
2 teaspoons brown sugar
1 teaspoon grated fresh ginger
1 clove garlic, crushed

Combine pork and marinade in bowl, cover, refrigerate 3 hours or overnight.

Remove steaks from marinade, reserve marinade. Heat oil in pan, add pork, cook until well browned, add reserved marinade. Bring to boil, simmer, covered, about 5 minutes or until pork is cooked through. Serve pork with sauce. Serve with vegetables or salad, if desired.

Marinade: Combine all ingredients in bowl; mix well.

Serves 4.

■ Recipe can be prepared a day ahead.
■ Storage: Covered, in refrigerator.
■ Freeze: Marinated pork suitable.
■ Microwave: Suitable.

LEFT: From left: Pork with White Wine and Mushroom Sauce, Pork with Orange Ginger Sauce.

Plates from Villa Italiana; cloth from Accoutrement

APRICOT GLAZED RIBS

425g can apricot halves in syrup
2 tablespoons honey
2 tablespoons barbecue sauce
1 tablespoon light soy sauce
1 tablespoon chilli sauce
1 tablespoon white vinegar
1 small chicken stock cube, crumbled
2 cloves garlic, crushed
¼ teaspoon ground paprika
1½kg American-style pork ribs

Blend or process undrained apricots, honey, sauces, vinegar, stock cube, garlic and paprika until smooth.

Reserve half the apricot mixture; brush ribs with remaining mixture. Grill or barbecue ribs until tender, brushing occasionally with apricot mixture.

Heat reserved apricot mixture in pan, serve with ribs. Serve with noodles or rice and salad, if desired.

Serves 4.

■ Apricot glaze can be made a day ahead.
■ Storage: Covered, in refrigerator.
■ Freeze: Not suitable.
■ Microwave: Apricot glaze suitable.

PORK STIR-FRY WITH LYCHEES

565g can lychees in syrup
1 tablespoon oil
500g pork fillets, sliced
2 green shallots, chopped
100g snow peas
½ red pepper, chopped
3 teaspoons light soy sauce
½ cup dry sherry
1 tablespoon lime juice
½ teaspoon grated fresh ginger
1 tablespoon cornflour
1 tablespoon chopped fresh parsley

Drain lychees, reserve half cup of the syrup. Heat oil in wok or large pan, add pork, stir-fry until browned and tender. Add shallots, peas and pepper, stir-fry until vegetables are just tender. Stir in sauce, sherry, juice, ginger and blended cornflour and reserved lychee syrup. Stir until sauce boils and thickens. Add lychees, stir until heated through. Serve sprinkled with parsley. Serve with rice, if desired.

Serves 4.

■ Recipe best made just before serving.
■ Freeze: Not suitable.
■ Microwave: Not suitable.

CURRIED PORK AND APPLE RISOTTO

375g carton chicken stock
500g pork sausages
40g butter
1 large onion, chopped
1 clove garlic, crushed
2 teaspoons curry powder
1 cup long-grain rice
1 cup apple juice
1½ cups water
2 apples, peeled, diced
3 green shallots, chopped
¼ cup sultanas

Bring stock to boil in pan, add sausages, simmer, uncovered, 3 minutes. Drain sausages, reserve 1 cup of the stock. Cut sausages into rounds.

Meanwhile, heat butter in pan, add onion, garlic and curry powder, cook, stirring, until onion is soft. Stir in rice, cook, stirring, 1 minute. Stir in reserved stock, juice and water.

Bring to boil, simmer, covered, about 12 minutes or until liquid is absorbed. Add sausages, apples, shallots and sultanas, stir until apples are tender.

Serves 4.

■ Recipe best made just before serving.
■ Freeze: Suitable.
■ Microwave: Suitable.

LEFT: Pork Stir-Fry with Lychees, Apricot Glazed Ribs.
RIGHT: Curried Pork and Apple Risotto.

Left: Jug from Horgan Imports. Right: Cloth from Les Olivades

PORK WITH LEMON PEPPER GLAZE

600g pork fillets
40g butter

LEMON PEPPER GLAZE
2 tablespoons honey
½ cup water
½ small chicken stock cube, crumbled
1 teaspoon lemon pepper
2 teaspoons cornflour
¼ cup lemon juice

Cut pork into 2cm slices. Heat butter in pan, add pork, cook until tender. Serve with lemon pepper glaze. Serve with vegetables or salad, if desired.
Lemon Pepper Glaze: Combine honey, water, stock cube and pepper in pan, stir in blended cornflour and juice; stir over heat until glaze boils and thickens.

Serves 4.

- Lemon pepper glaze can be made a day ahead.
- Storage: Covered, in refrigerator.
- Freeze: Not suitable.
- Microwave: Suitable.

MILD CHILLI PORK WITH PEPPERS

1 tablespoon oil
4 pork butterfly steaks
1 tablespoon oil, extra
2 onions, sliced
1 clove garlic, crushed
1 teaspoon sambal oelek
1 red pepper, chopped
1 green pepper, chopped
1 yellow pepper, chopped
400ml can coconut milk
1 tablespoon cornflour
½ cup water
2 small chicken stock cubes, crumbled
1 teaspoon sugar

Heat oil in pan, add pork, cook until well browned and tender; remove pork from pan, drain pan.

Heat extra oil in pan, add onions, garlic, sambal oelek and peppers, cook, stirring, until onion is soft. Stir in coconut milk, blended cornflour and water, stock cubes and sugar; stir until mixture boils and thickens. Return pork to pan, cook until heated through. Serve with rice, if desired.

Serves 4.

- Recipe best made just before serving.
- Freeze: Not suitable.
- Microwave: Suitable.

PORK WITH ANCHOVY AND PINE NUT SAUCE

1 tablespoon oil
4 pork chops
2 cloves garlic, crushed
200g baby mushrooms, sliced
1 tomato, seeded, chopped
45g can anchovy fillets, drained, chopped
¼ cup pine nuts
½ cup dry red wine
½ cup water
1 teaspoon sugar
1 tablespoon white vinegar
60g butter, chopped
2 tablespoons chopped fresh parsley

Heat oil in large pan, add pork, cook until lightly browned and cooked through; remove pork from pan.

Add garlic, mushrooms, tomato and anchovies to pan, cook, stirring, until mushrooms are soft. Stir in nuts, wine, water, sugar and vinegar; bring to boil, simmer, uncovered, 10 minutes. Remove pan from heat, quickly stir in butter and parsley. Serve sauce over pork. Serve with vegetables or salad, if desired.

Serves 4.

- Recipe best made just before serving.
- Freeze: Not suitable.
- Microwave: Not suitable.

LEFT: Clockwise from left: Pork with Lemon Pepper Glaze, Mild Chilli Pork with Peppers, Pork with Anchovy and Pine Nut Sauce.

Plates from Amy's Tableware and Villa Italiana

HAM AND PEPPERONI PIZZA

8 slices ham
½ cup tomato paste
½ cup tomato sauce
4 Lebanese bread rounds
100g sliced pepperoni salami
1 green pepper, sliced
80g baby mushrooms, sliced
1 teaspoon dried oregano leaves
4 cups (400g) grated
 mozzarella cheese
1 tablespoon chopped fresh parsley

Slice ham into thin strips. Combine paste and sauce in bowl. Spread sauce mixture over bread rounds, top with ham, pepperoni, pepper, mushrooms, oregano and cheese. Sprinkle with parsley.

Place pizzas on oven trays, bake in hot oven about 10 minutes or until pizzas are browned. Serve with salad, if desired.

Serves 4.

■ Recipe best made just before serving.
■ Freeze: Not suitable.
■ Microwave: Not suitable.

SPAGHETTI WITH THREE PEPPERS AND HAM

500g spaghetti pasta
1 tablespoon oil
1 small onion, chopped
1 red pepper, sliced
1 green pepper, sliced
1 yellow pepper, sliced
2 cloves garlic, crushed
410g can tomatoes
½ teaspoon sugar
2 tablespoons tomato paste
200g ham, chopped
½ teaspoon cracked black
 peppercorns
⅓ cup shredded fresh basil

Add pasta to large pan of boiling water, boil, uncovered, until just tender; drain.

Meanwhile, heat oil in pan, add onion, peppers and garlic, cook, stirring, until onion is soft. Add undrained crushed tomatoes, sugar, paste, ham and peppercorns; bring to boil, simmer, uncovered, 5 minutes. Stir in basil. Serve sauce over pasta. Serve with salad, if desired.

Serves 4.

■ Sauce can be made a day ahead.
■ Storage: Covered, in refrigerator.
■ Freeze: Sauce suitable.
■ Microwave: Suitable.

WARM PORK SALAD WITH RED CABBAGE

600g pork fillets
80g sliced ham
2 tablespoons oil
1 large onion, sliced
2 teaspoons sugar
1 tablespoon marmalade
⅓ cup dry sherry
¼ cup chopped dried apricots
2 tablespoons red wine vinegar
¼ medium red cabbage, shredded

Cut pork in half lengthways. Cut ham into thin strips.

Heat oil in pan, add pork, cook until browned and tender; drain on absorbent paper, cut into slices.

Add onion and sugar to pan, cook, stirring, until onion is soft. Stir in ham, marmalade, sherry and apricots. Bring to boil, simmer, uncovered, until 2 tablespoons of liquid remain in pan; stir in vinegar and pork. Serve pork mixture over cabbage.

Serves 4.

■ Recipe can be made a day ahead and served cold.
■ Storage: Covered, in refrigerator.
■ Freeze: Not suitable.
■ Microwave: Not suitable.

LEFT: From top: Spaghetti with Three Peppers and Ham, Ham and Pepperoni Pizza. RIGHT: Warm Pork Salad with Red Cabbage.

Left: Platter from Corso de Fiori. Right: Bowl from Corso de Fiori

PORK WITH GARLIC AND MUSHROOM SAUCE

4 pork chops
plain flour
2 tablespoons oil

GARLIC AND MUSHROOM SAUCE
60g butter
4 cloves garlic, crushed
350g baby mushrooms, quartered
⅓ cup sweet sherry
6 green shallots, sliced
2 teaspoons cornflour
⅔ cup water
¼ teaspoon dried dill tips

Toss pork in flour, shake away excess flour. Heat oil in pan, cook pork until well browned and cooked through; drain on absorbent paper. Serve pork with garlic and mushroom sauce. Serve with vegetables or salad, if desired.
Garlic and Mushroom Sauce: Heat butter in pan, add garlic and mushrooms, cook, stirring, until mushrooms are tender, add sherry. Bring to boil, simmer, uncovered, until reduced by half. Add shallots and blended cornflour and water, stir until sauce boils and thickens, stir in dill.

Serves 4.

- Sauce can be made a day ahead.
- Storage: Covered, in refrigerator.
- Freeze: Not suitable.
- Microwave: Sauce suitable.

TORTELLINI WITH CREAMY BACON SAUCE

500g tortellini
1 tablespoon olive oil
4 bacon rashers, chopped
4 green shallots, chopped
¼ cup drained sun-dried tomatoes, chopped
½ cup cream
½ cup sour cream
¼ cup water
½ cup grated parmesan cheese
1 tablespoon chopped fresh basil

Add tortellini to large pan of boiling water, boil, uncovered, until just tender; drain.
Meanwhile, heat oil in pan, add bacon, cook, stirring, until bacon is crisp. Add shallots and tomatoes, cook, stirring, until shallots are just tender; remove and reserve half the bacon mixture for serving.
Stir cream, sour cream, water, cheese and basil into remaining bacon mixture in pan; stir until heated through. Combine tortellini and cream mixture, toss well. Serve sprinkled with reserved bacon mixture. Serve with salad, if desired.

Serves 4.

- Recipe best made just before serving.
- Freeze: Not suitable.
- Microwave: Suitable.

❖ DEVILLED PORK SPARE RIBS

8 racks (about 2kg) American-style spare ribs
425g can tomato puree
2 tablespoons Worcestershire sauce
2 teaspoons dry mustard
1 onion, finely chopped
¼ cup brown sugar
½ cup brown vinegar
½ cup oil

Combine all ingredients in bowl, cover, refrigerate several hours or overnight, turning ribs occasionally.
Place ribs on rack in baking dish, bake in hot oven about 20 minutes or until pork is tender. Serve with vegetables or salad, if desired.

Serves 4.

- Recipe can be prepared a day ahead.
- Storage: Covered, in refrigerator.
- Freeze: Not suitable.
- Microwave: Not suitable.

RIGHT: Clockwise from top left: Devilled Pork Spare Ribs, Tortellini with Creamy Bacon Sauce, Pork with Garlic and Mushroom Sauce.

Plates from Amy's Tableware

SPICY PORK AND APRICOT CURRY

1 tablespoon oil
500g pork fillets, sliced
1 onion, sliced
2 teaspoons vindaloo curry paste
1 cup water
2/3 cup dried apricots, sliced
1 tablespoon chopped fresh coriander
2 teaspoons cornflour
2 teaspoons lime juice
1/4 cup sour cream

Heat oil in large pan or wok, add pork, stir-fry until well browned. Add onion, stir-fry until onion is soft. Stir in paste, water, apricots and coriander; bring to boil, simmer, covered, about 5 minutes or until pork is tender. Stir in blended cornflour and juice, stir until mixture boils and thickens; stir in cream. Serve curry with rice, if desired.

Serves 4.

■ Recipe best made just before serving.
■ Freeze: Not suitable.
■ Microwave: Not suitable.

PORK WITH LEEK AND RAISIN CONSERVE

2 tablespoons oil
4 pork steaks

LEEK AND RAISIN CONSERVE
30g butter
1 medium leek, sliced
1/2 cup raisins
1/4 cup sugar
1/4 cup white vinegar
1/2 teaspoon grated orange rind
1/4 cup orange juice
2 tablespoons water

Heat oil in pan, add pork, cook on both sides until well browned and cooked through. Serve with leek and raisin conserve. Serve with vegetables, if desired.
Leek and Raisin Conserve: Heat butter in pan, add leek, cook, stirring, until leek is soft. Add raisins, sugar, vinegar, rind, juice and water, stir over heat, without boiling, until sugar is dissolved. Bring to boil, simmer, uncovered, about 10 minutes, stirring occasionally, or until thickened slightly.

Serves 4.

■ Conserve can be made a week ahead.
■ Storage: Covered, in refrigerator.
■ Freeze: Not suitable.
■ Microwave: Conserve suitable.

FRIED RICE WITH BACON AND VEGETABLES

1 tablespoon oil
8 bacon rashers, chopped
4 eggs, lightly beaten
1 teaspoon cracked black peppercorns
1 tablespoon oil, extra
250g mushrooms, chopped
100g snow peas
1 red pepper, chopped
4 cups cooked rice
6 green shallots, chopped
2 tablespoons light soy sauce
1 small chicken stock cube, crumbled

Heat oil in large pan or wok, add bacon, cook, stirring, until crisp; drain on absorbent paper. Add eggs and peppercorns to pan, cook until omelette is lightly browned underneath. Turn omelette, brown other side, remove omelette from pan, cut omelette into thin strips.

Heat extra oil in pan, add mushrooms, peas and pepper, cook, stirring, until vegetables are just tender. Stir in bacon, omelette strips, rice, shallots and combined sauce and stock cube; stir over heat until mixture is heated through.

Serves 4.

■ Recipe best made just before serving.
■ Freeze: Suitable.
■ Microwave: Suitable.

SWEET AND SOUR PORK WITH CUCUMBER

1 onion
2 tablespoons oil
600g pork fillets, sliced
2 small green cucumbers, sliced
1 red pepper, sliced
1 teaspoon grated fresh ginger
55g packet sweet and sour sauce mix
1/2 teaspoon five spice powder
3/4 cup water

Slice onion into wedges. Heat oil in wok or large pan, add pork, stir-fry until browned and tender. Add onion, cucumbers and pepper, stir-fry until onion is just soft. Stir in ginger, sauce mix, five spice powder and water. Stir over heat until sauce boils and thickens. Serve with noodles or rice, if desired.

Serves 4.

■ Recipe best made just before serving.
■ Freeze: Not suitable.
■ Microwave: Suitable.

LEFT: From top: Pork with Leek and Raisin Conserve, Spicy Pork and Apricot Curry. RIGHT: From top: Sweet and Sour Pork with Cucumber, Fried Rice with Bacon and Vegetables.

Left: Plates from Villa Italiana. Right: Plate and cutlery from Accoutrement

ALMOND PORK WITH FRUITY SAUCE

2 (about 600g) pork fillets
plain flour
1 tablespoon milk
2 eggs, lightly beaten
3 cups (240g) flaked almonds
¼ cup packaged breadcrumbs
¼ cup oil

FRUITY SAUCE
100g prosciutto
2 tablespoons oil
2 onions, sliced
1 large apple, peeled, sliced
¼ teaspoon ground cinnamon
1 tablespoon teriyaki sauce
1½ cups orange juice
1 tablespoon chopped fresh parsley

Cut each fillet into 4 pieces, place pieces between sheets of plastic wrap, flatten gently with meat mallet. Toss pork in flour, shake away excess flour, dip into combined milk and eggs, toss in combined nuts and crumbs; press coating on firmly.

Heat oil in pan, add pork, cook until lightly browned and tender; drain on absorbent paper. Serve fruity sauce over pork. Serve with beans, salad or vegetables, if desired.

Fruity Sauce: Cut prosciutto into thin strips. Heat oil in pan, add onions and apple, cook, stirring, until onion is soft, add prosciutto, cinnamon, sauce and juice. Bring to boil, simmer, uncovered, about 2 minutes or until apple is soft; stir in parsley.

Serves 4.

■ Recipe can be prepared a day ahead.
■ Storage: Covered, in refrigerator.
■ Freeze: Uncooked crumbed pork suitable.
■ Microwave: Sauce suitable.

TASTY PEPPERONI PASTA

500g fettucine pasta
1 tablespoon olive oil
1 onion, chopped
1 clove garlic, crushed
3 bacon rashers, chopped
1 stick pepperoni sausage, sliced
2 sticks cabanossi, sliced
300ml carton cream
¼ cup chopped fresh basil
1 tablespoon chopped fresh chives
¼ cup grated parmesan cheese

Add pasta to large pan of boiling water, boil, uncovered until just tender; drain.

Meanwhile, heat oil in pan, add onion, garlic, bacon, pepperoni and cabanossi, cook, stirring, until onion is soft. Stir in cream, bring to boil, stir in herbs and cheese. Toss sauce through pasta. Serve with salad, if desired.

Serves 4.

■ Sauce can be made a day ahead.
■ Storage: Covered, in refrigerator.
■ Freeze: Not suitable.
■ Microwave: Suitable.

BUTTERFLY PORK WITH SHALLOTS AND CAPERS

20g butter
1 tablespoon oil
4 pork butterfly steaks
1 teaspoon seasoned pepper
1 clove garlic, crushed
6 green shallots, chopped
2 tablespoons drained capers
2 tablespoons dry white wine
1 small chicken stock cube, crumbled
½ cup water
1 teaspoon cornflour
3 teaspoons water, extra
½ cup sour cream

Heat butter and oil in pan, add pork, cook until tender; remove pork from pan.

Add pepper, garlic and shallots to pan, cook, stirring, until shallots are just tender. Stir in capers, wine, stock cube, water and blended cornflour and extra water. Stir until mixture boils and thickens. Stir in cream; serve over pork. Serve with vegetables or salad, if desired.

Serves 4.

■ Recipe best made just before serving.
■ Freeze: Not suitable.
■ Microwave: Suitable.

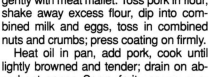

LEFT: Almond Pork with Fruity Sauce.
RIGHT: From left: Tasty Pepperoni Pasta, Butterfly Pork with Shallots and Capers.

Left: China from Horgan Imports; cutlery from Jarass
Right: China from J.D. Milner & Associates

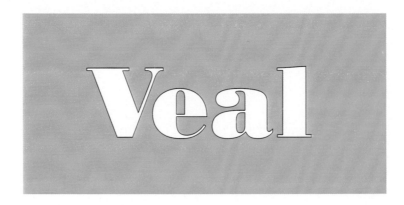

Veal

■ *Delicate veal needs gentle cooking, particularly when grilling or frying. First seal the outside on high heat then reduce heat to cook gently until tender.* ■ *Unlike most other meats, veal has very little fat and dries out quickly without the use of oil or butter.* ■ *When suitable, pound veal steaks to an even thickness as this helps them to cook evenly.* ■ *Microwaved veal is very pale, so use a browning plate for good results.* ■ *You can substitute one cut for another where suitable, if you prefer.* ■ *Marinated recipes are indicated by this symbol ❖ this means you need to start ahead of time.*

VEAL WITH VEGETABLE STIR-FRY AND MINT CREAM

8 veal cutlets
50g butter, melted
2 tablespoons chopped fresh mint
1 tablespoon oil
1 carrot, grated
2 medium (about 200g) zucchini, grated
½ cup sour cream
1 tablespoon water

Brush veal with combined butter and mint, reserve remaining butter mixture. Grill veal until tender.

Meanwhile, heat oil in pan, add vegetables, stir-fry until just tender. Combine reserved butter mixture, sour cream and water in pan, stir over heat until heated through.

Serve veal over vegetables, topped with sauce. Serve with extra vegetables or rice, if desired.

Serves 4.

■ Recipe best made just before serving.
■ Freeze: Not suitable.
■ Microwave: Not suitable.

CRUMBED VEAL WITH EGG AND ANCHOVY BUTTER

1 cup (100g) packaged breadcrumbs
2 tablespoons chopped fresh parsley
1 small beef stock cube, crumbled
8 veal cutlets
plain flour
1 egg, lightly beaten
2 tablespoons milk
oil for shallow-frying

EGG AND ANCHOVY BUTTER
1 hard-boiled egg, roughly chopped
3 canned drained anchovy fillets, chopped
125g butter, softened
2 teaspoons lemon juice
½ teaspoon cracked black peppercorns
1 tablespoon finely chopped red pepper

Combine breadcrumbs, parsley and stock cube in bowl. Toss veal in flour, shake away excess flour. Dip veal into combined egg and milk, toss in breadcrumb mixture. Shallow-fry veal in hot oil until browned and tender; drain on absorbent paper. Serve veal with egg and anchovy butter.

Serve with vegetables, if desired.

Egg and Anchovy Butter: Blend or process egg, anchovies, butter, juice and peppercorns until well combined. Transfer mixture to bowl, add pepper; mix well. Roll mixture into a log shape, wrap in foil, freeze until firm.

Serves 4.

■ Veal can be prepared a day ahead. Egg and anchovy butter can be made 2 days ahead.
■ Storage: Covered, in refrigerator.
■ Freeze: Uncooked crumbed veal and egg and anchovy butter suitable.
■ Microwave: Not suitable.

RIGHT: Crumbed Veal with Egg and Anchovy Butter, Veal with Vegetable Stir-Fry and Mint Cream.

China from Villeroy & Boch; cloth from Boyac

VEAL WITH SALMON AND MANGO SAUCE

600g loin of veal, boned
2 slices smoked salmon
4 bacon rashers
2 tablespoons oil

MANGO SAUCE
½ cup chopped mango
½ cup cream
¼ cup dry white wine
1 tablespoon chopped fresh chives

Cut veal crossways into 4 thick steaks; flatten steaks slightly Cut a pocket in side of each steak, fill with half a slice of salmon. Wrap bacon around each steak, secure with toothpicks. Heat oil in pan, add steaks, cook until tender, serve with mango sauce and vegetables, if desired.
Mango Sauce: Blend or process mango until smooth. Combine mango puree, cream and wine in pan, stir over heat until heated through; stir in chives.

Serves 4.

- ■ Sauce can be made a day ahead.
- ■ Storage: Covered, in refrigerator.
- ■ Freeze: Uncooked filled veal suitable.
- ■ Microwave: Sauce suitable.

VEAL WITH CHEESE AND SALAMI CRUST

2 tablespoons olive oil
4 veal chops
2 cloves garlic, crushed
3 green shallots, chopped
1 tablespoon olive paste
180g sliced Calabrese salami
¼ cup drained sun-dried
**   tomatoes, sliced**
200g mozzarella cheese, sliced

Heat oil in pan, add veal, cook until browned and tender; remove veal from pan. Pour away excess oil, leaving 1 tablespoon in pan. Add garlic and shallots to pan, cook, stirring, until shallots are soft. Add paste, salami and tomatoes.

Place veal on oven tray, top with salami mixture, sprinkle with cheese. Grill until cheese is melted and lightly browned. Serve with vegetables or salad, if desired.

Serves 4.

- ■ Recipe best made just before serving.
- ■ Freeze: Not suitable.
- ■ Microwave: Not suitable.

VEAL WITH MUSTARD SAUCE

1 tablespoon oil
4 veal steaks
20g butter
3 green shallots, chopped
2 tablespoons French mustard
300ml carton thickened cream
2 tablespoons chopped fresh chives

Heat oil in pan, add veal, cook until browned and tender; remove veal from pan. Melt butter in same pan, add shallots, cook, stirring, until soft, add mustard, cream and half the chives. Bring to boil, simmer, uncovered, until sauce is slightly thickened, serve over veal, sprinkle with remaining chives. Serve with vegetables or salad, if desired.

Serves 4.

- ■ Recipe best made just before serving.
- ■ Freeze: Not suitable.
- ■ Microwave: Suitable.

BELOW: Veal with Salmon and Mango Sauce.
RIGHT: From top: Veal with Mustard Sauce, Veal with Cheese and Salami Crust.

Below: China from Royal Doulton; cloth from Boyac. Right: Plates from Amy's Tableware; cloth from Boyac

ALMOND VEAL WITH CREAMY LEMON SAUCE

4 veal leg steaks
plain flour
2 eggs, lightly beaten
1 cup (100g) packaged breadcrumbs
2 teaspoons grated lemon rind
½ cup packaged ground almonds
1 teaspoon cracked black
     peppercorns
oil for shallow-frying

CREAMY LEMON SAUCE
300ml carton thickened cream
¼ cup lemon juice
1 teaspoon seeded mustard
½ teaspoon sugar
2 teaspoons cornflour
2 teaspoons water

Toss veal in flour, shake away excess flour, dip into eggs, toss in combined breadcrumbs, rind, nuts and peppercorns; shake away excess crumb mixture.

Shallow-fry veal in hot oil until lightly browned and cooked through. Serve with creamy lemon sauce. Serve with vegetables, if desired.
Creamy Lemon Sauce: Combine cream, juice, mustard and sugar in pan, stir in blended cornflour and water, stir over heat until sauce boils and thickens.

Serves 4.

- Recipe can be prepared a day ahead.
- Storage: Covered, in refrigerator.
- Freeze: Not suitable.
- Microwave: Sauce suitable.

VEAL MEDALLIONS WITH SUN-DRIED TOMATOES

1 tablespoon olive oil
8 veal medallions
4 green shallots, chopped
½ cup drained sun-dried
     tomatoes, sliced
1 tablespoon drained capers
2 tablespoons dry white wine
1 small chicken stock cube, crumbled
¼ cup water
1 teaspoon dried thyme leaves
1 tablespoon chopped fresh basil
90g butter, chopped

Heat oil in pan, add veal, cook until well browned. Transfer to baking dish, cover, bake in moderately hot oven about 10 minutes or until tender.

Reheat same pan, add shallots, tomatoes, capers, wine, stock cube, water and herbs. Bring to boil, remove pan from heat, quickly whisk in butter, a few pieces at a time, until sauce is thickened. Serve sauce with veal. Serve with vegetables or pasta, if desired.

Serves 4.

- Recipe best made just before serving.
- Freeze: Not suitable.
- Microwave: Not suitable.

❖ VEAL WITH SPICY CARROT CREAM

2 cloves garlic, crushed
½ teaspoon dried rosemary leaves
¼ cup olive oil
2 tablespoons lemon juice
8 veal chops

SPICY CARROT CREAM
440g can baby carrots, drained
½ teaspoon ground cumin
¼ teaspoon ground coriander

Combine garlic, rosemary, oil and juice in bowl; reserve 2 tablespoons of marinade for spicy carrot cream. Add veal to marinade in bowl, cover, refrigerate several hours or overnight.

Grill veal until browned and tender. Serve with spicy carrot cream.
Spicy Carrot Cream: Combine reserved marinade, carrots and spices in pan, bring to boil. Blend or process until smooth.

Serves 4.

- Recipe can be prepared a day ahead.
- Storage: Covered, in refrigerator.
- Freeze: Not suitable.
- Microwave: Sauce suitable.

LEFT: Clockwise from top left: Almond Veal with Creamy Lemon Sauce, Veal with Spicy Carrot Cream, Veal Medallions with Sun-Dried Tomatoes.

China from Royal Doulton; cloth from Boyac

VEAL PARMESAN

20g butter
1 tablespoon olive oil
4 veal steaks
150g baby mushrooms, quartered
1 cup spaghetti sauce
1 tablespoon chopped fresh basil
1 cup (100g) grated mozzarella cheese
½ cup grated parmesan cheese

Heat butter and oil in pan, add veal, cook until lightly browned and tender. Transfer to shallow flameproof dish.

Reheat pan, add mushrooms, cook, stirring, until mushrooms are tender. Stir in spaghetti sauce, cook until heated through. Spoon sauce mixture over veal, top with combined basil and cheeses. Grill until cheeses are melted and lightly browned. Serve with pasta, vegetables or salad, if desired.

Serves 4.

- Recipe can be prepared 3 hours ahead.
- Storage: Covered, in refrigerator.
- Freeze: Suitable.
- Microwave: Not suitable.

VEAL AND ARTICHOKE RAGOUT

¼ cup oil
600g veal steak, sliced
1 onion, finely chopped
2 cloves garlic, crushed
½ cup tomato paste
2 teaspoons paprika
300g can Mushroom Supreme
275g can artichoke hearts in oil, drained, halved
390g can red pimientos, drained, sliced
1 teaspoon sugar
½ cup water
¼ cup chopped fresh parsley

Heat oil in pan, add veal, cook, stirring, until lightly browned. Add onion and garlic, cook, stirring, until onion is soft. Stir in paste and paprika, cook, stirring, until combined. Add Mushroom Supreme, artichokes, pimientos, sugar and water to pan, bring to boil, simmer, uncovered, until thickened; stir in parsley. Serve with pasta or rice, if desired.

Serves 4.

- Recipe can be made a day ahead.
- Storage: Covered, in refrigerator.
- Freeze: Not suitable.
- Microwave: Not suitable.

VEAL WITH PROSCIUTTO AND PROVOLONE

30g butter
4 veal leg steaks
½ cup marsala
125g mushrooms, sliced
1 small chicken stock cube, crumbled
2 teaspoons cornflour
2 teaspoons water
4 slices prosciutto
½ cup grated provolone cheese

Heat butter in large pan, add veal, cook until tender; remove veal from pan. Add marsala, mushrooms and stock cube to pan, bring to boil, simmer, uncovered, 1 minute. Stir in blended cornflour and water, stir until mixture boils and thickens.

Place veal on oven tray, top with prosciutto, spoon over mushroom mixture, sprinkle with cheese. Grill until cheese is melted. Serve veal with pasta and salad, if desired.

Serves 4.

- Recipe best made just before serving.
- Freeze: Not suitable.
- Microwave: Not suitable.

LEFT: From top: Veal Parmesan, Veal and Artichoke Ragout.
ABOVE: Veal with Prosciutto and Provolone.

Left: Fabric from Boyac

FETTUCINE WITH VEAL AND EGGPLANT SAUCE

250g spinach fettucine pasta
1 tablespoon olive oil
1 clove garlic, crushed
2 medium leeks, sliced
¼ cup olive oil, extra
500g veal leg steaks, sliced
1 medium (about 300g) eggplant,
    chopped
1 small red pepper, sliced
4 thick slices prosciutto, sliced
300ml carton cream
½ cup milk
2 teaspoons seeded mustard
2 tablespoons chopped fresh chives

Add pasta to large pan of boiling water, boil, uncovered, until just tender; drain.

Meanwhile, heat oil in large pan or wok, add garlic and leeks, stir-fry until leeks are soft; remove leek mixture from pan.

Add extra oil to pan, add veal and eggplant, stir-fry until veal is well browned. Add pepper and prosciutto, stir-fry until pepper is tender. Stir in leek mixture, cream, milk, mustard and chives, stir until mixture boils. Serve sauce over pasta.

Serves 4.

■ Recipe best made just before serving.
■ Freeze: Not suitable.
■ Microwave: Pasta suitable.

VEAL WITH CRISP BACON AND ORANGE SAUCE

2 bacon rashers, chopped
8 veal cutlets
2 teaspoons lemon pepper

ORANGE SAUCE
30g butter
2 small leeks, chopped
1 tablespoon plain flour
⅓ cup orange juice
1½ tablespoons lemon juice
¼ cup water
1 teaspoon sugar
80g butter, chopped, extra

VEAL WITH CREAMY BAKED POTATOES

**2 large (about 400g) potatoes,
  thinly sliced**
1 onion, sliced
½ cup cream
½ cup grated parmesan cheese
8 veal steaks
plain flour
2 eggs, lightly beaten
¼ cup olive oil

TOMATO SAUCE
410g can tomatoes
½ teaspoon dried mixed herbs
1 teaspoon castor sugar
1 small beef stock cube, crumbled

Lightly grease 23cm pie plate. Add potatoes and onion to pan of simmering water, bring to boil, drain. Combine potatoes, onion, cream and cheese in bowl, spoon into prepared plate. Bake, uncovered, in hot oven 20 minutes.

Meanwhile, toss veal in flour, shake away excess flour, dip into eggs. Heat oil in pan, add veal, cook until tender; drain on absorbent paper. Serve veal with creamy potatoes and tomato sauce.

Tomato Sauce: Blend or process undrained tomatoes until smooth. Combine tomatoes and remaining ingredients in pan, bring to boil, simmer, uncovered, until thickened slightly.

Serves 4.

- Tomato sauce can be made 2 days ahead.
- Storage: Covered, in refrigerator.
- Freeze: Sauce suitable.
- Microwave: Sauce and potatoes suitable.

LEFT: From left: Veal with Crisp Bacon and Orange Sauce, Fettucine with Veal and Eggplant Sauce.
BELOW: Veal with Creamy Baked Potatoes.

Left and below: Plates from Incorporated Agencies

Cook bacon in pan until crisp; drain. Rub veal with lemon pepper, grill until browned and tender. Serve veal with orange sauce; sprinkle with bacon. Serve with pasta or vegetables, if desired.

Orange Sauce: Heat butter in pan, add leeks, cook, stirring, until soft, add flour, stir until mixture is dry and grainy. Remove from heat, gradually stir in juices, water and sugar, stir over heat until mixture boils and thickens. Remove from heat, quickly whisk in extra butter.

Serves 4.

- Recipe best made just before serving.
- Freeze: Not suitable.
- Microwave: Not suitable.

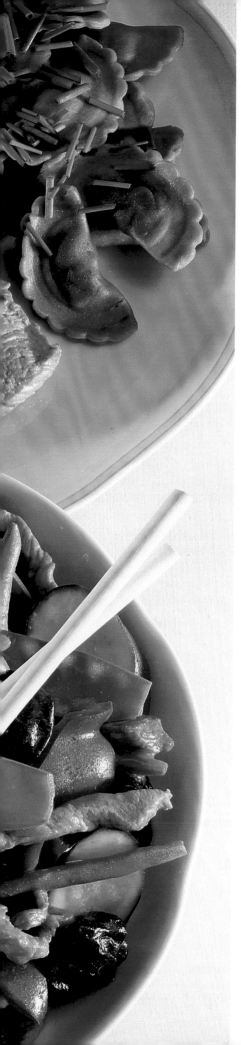

GINGER VEAL STIR-FRY

2 tablespoons oil
4 veal steaks, sliced
1 tablespoon oil, extra
2 medium (about 200g) zucchini,
  sliced
100g snow peas
100g green beans
1 red pepper, chopped
⅔ cup pitted prunes
¼ cup dry sherry
1 teaspoon dark soy sauce
2 teaspoons lime juice
½ teaspoon ground ginger
1 tablespoon sugar
1½ tablespoons cornflour
¼ cup water

Heat oil in large pan or wok, add veal, stir-fry until well browned; remove veal from pan. Add extra oil to pan, add vegetables and prunes, stir-fry until vegetables are just tender. Stir in sherry, sauce, juice, ginger, sugar and blended cornflour and water, stir until mixture boils and thickens. Return veal to pan, stir until heated through. Serve with rice, if desired.
Serves 4.

■ Recipe best made just before serving.
■ Freeze: Not suitable.
■ Microwave: Not suitable.

VEAL WITH RED PEPPER AND CORN COMPOTE

4 veal chops

RED PEPPER AND CORN COMPOTE
30g butter
1 red pepper, finely sliced
1 onion, finely chopped
1 tablespoon chopped fresh
  lemon grass
310g can corn kernels, drained
¾ cup water
⅓ cup white vinegar
½ cup brown sugar, firmly packed
2 teaspoons cornflour
1 tablespoon water, extra

Grill veal until cooked through. Serve with red pepper compote. Serve with noodles, pasta or salad, if desired.
Red Pepper and Corn Compote: Heat butter in pan, add pepper, onion, lemon grass and corn, cook, stirring, 1 minute. Add water and vinegar, bring to boil, simmer, uncovered, 2 minutes or until pepper is soft. Add sugar, stir until dissolved. Stir in blended cornflour and extra water, stir over heat until mixture boils and thickens.
Serves 4.

■ Red pepper and corn compote can be made a week ahead.
■ Storage: Covered, in refrigerator.
■ Freeze: Not suitable.
■ Microwave: Red pepper and corn compote suitable.

VEAL MARSALA

2 tablespoons oil
4 veal steaks
1 onion, chopped
250g mushrooms, sliced
¼ cup marsala
2 teaspoons cornflour
⅔ cup water
1 small chicken stock cube, crumbled
1 tablespoon chopped fresh chives

Heat oil in pan, add veal, cook until lightly browned and tender; remove veal from pan. Add onion to pan, cook, stirring, until soft. Add mushrooms, marsala, blended cornflour and water, and stock cube. Stir over heat until mixture boils and thickens; stir in chives. Serve sauce over veal. Serve with pasta or vegetables, if desired.
Serves 4.

■ Recipe best made just before serving.
■ Freeze: Not suitable.
■ Microwave: Not suitable.

LEFT: Clockwise from left: Veal with Red Pepper and Corn Compote, Veal Marsala, Ginger Veal Stir-Fry.

Plates from Incorporated Agencies

VEAL WITH SNOW PEAS AND ASPARAGUS

50g butter
1 tablespoon oil
2 cloves garlic, crushed
4 veal steaks
4 green shallots, sliced
1 medium bunch (12 spears) fresh asparagus, chopped
200g snow peas
250g punnet cherry tomatoes
2 teaspoons cornflour
½ cup water
1 small chicken stock cube, crumbled

Heat butter, oil and garlic in pan, add veal, cook until lightly browned and tender; remove veal from pan. Add shallots, asparagus, peas and tomatoes to pan, cook, stirring, 1 minute. Stir in blended cornflour and water, and stock cube, stir over heat until mixture boils and thickens slightly. Serve vegetables over veal. Serve with salad, if desired.

Serves 4.

■ Recipe best made just before serving.
■ Freeze: Not suitable.
■ Microwave: Not suitable.

ABOVE: Veal with Snow Peas and Asparagus.
RIGHT: Veal Parcels with Leek and Pimientos.

Above: Plate from Villa Italiana; napkin from Les Olivades. Right: Plate from Incorporated Agencies

VEAL PARCELS WITH LEEK AND PIMIENTOS

½ avocado
4 veal leg steaks
8 slices prosciutto
¼ cup oil
1 medium leek, sliced
390g can red pimientos,
    drained, sliced
¼ cup brown sugar
2 tablespoons brown vinegar

Cut avocado into 4 pieces, place a piece on each veal steak, fold over to enclose avocado. Wrap prosciutto around veal, secure with skewers.

Heat oil in large pan, cook parcels until browned and tender; remove parcels from pan. Add leek and pimientos to pan, cook, stirring, until leek is soft. Add sugar and vinegar, stir over heat, without boiling, until sugar is dissolved, serve over veal. Serve with pasta or rice, if desired.
Serves 4.

■ Recipe can be prepared a day ahead.
■ Storage: Covered, in refrigerator.
■ Freeze: Not suitable.
■ Microwave: Not suitable.

Seafood

■ *These recipes are extra quick because seafood requires so little cooking.* ■ *Where we have used fish fillets and cutlets, we have mostly left it to you to make your own choice of the type of fish, depending on your taste.* ■ *Don't overlook the cheaper types of fish as they will still suit our recipes and be just as tasty.* ■ *Take care not to overcook seafood as it quickly dries out and will not give the tempting results we intended.* ■ *Fish cooks well in the microwave oven, but take special care with timing.* ■ *As well as fillets and cutlets, we have used prawns, smoked salmon, scallops, tuna and more to give you a selection for all occasions.* ■ *Marinated recipes are indicated by this symbol* ❖ *this means you need to start ahead of time.*

GRILLED FISH WITH HERBED MAYONNAISE

4 white fish fillets

HERBED MAYONNAISE
½ cup mayonnaise
½ cup plain yogurt
1 tablespoon lemon juice
¼ cup chopped fresh watercress
2 tablespoons chopped fresh parsley
½ teaspoon dried dill tips
**1 teaspoon cracked black
    peppercorns**
1 teaspoon seeded mustard

Barbecue or grill fish until tender. Serve with herbed mayonnaise. Serve with salad, if desired.
Herbed Mayonnaise: Combine all ingredients in bowl; mix well.
Serves 4.
■ Herbed mayonnaise can be prepared a day ahead.
■ Storage: Covered, in refrigerator.
■ Freeze: Not suitable.
■ Microwave: Not suitable.

MUSSELS WITH GARLIC AND TOMATO SAUCE

1½kg large mussels
1 cup water

GARLIC AND TOMATO SAUCE
2 tablespoons olive oil
1 onion, finely chopped
6 cloves garlic, crushed
1 green pepper, finely chopped
100g mushrooms, chopped
1 teaspoon dried oregano leaves
410g can tomatoes
425g can tomato puree
1 cup water

Scrub mussels, remove beards. Heat water in large pan, add mussels, cook, covered, over high heat about 5 minutes or until mussels open. Drain mussels; discard liquid. Stir mussels into garlic and tomato sauce. Serve with bread and salad, if desired.
Garlic and Tomato Sauce: Heat oil in pan, add onion and garlic, cook, stirring, until onion is soft. Add pepper and mushrooms, cook, stirring, until vegetables are tender. Stir in oregano, undrained crushed tomatoes, puree and water, bring to boil, simmer, uncovered, until sauce is slightly thickened.
Serves 4.
■ Garlic and tomato sauce can be made a day ahead.
■ Storage: Covered, in refrigerator.
■ Freeze: Not suitable.
■ Microwave: Suitable.

RIGHT: From left: Grilled Fish with Herbed Mayonnaise, Mussels with Garlic and Tomato Sauce.

China from Villeroy & Boch

PRAWNS WITH HOT SPICY PESTO

1kg uncooked king prawns
2 onions
2 tablespoons oil
300g (3 cups) bean sprouts

HOT SPICY PESTO
¼ cup chopped fresh basil
2 tablespoons chopped fresh coriander
¼ cup oil
2 teaspoons sambal oelek
4 cloves garlic, crushed
1 teaspoon grated fresh ginger
2 tablespoons dry sherry
1 teaspoon sesame oil

Shell and devein prawns, leaving tails intact. Combine prawns and hot spicy pesto in bowl. Cut onions into wedges. Heat oil in large pan or wok, stir-fry onions until just tender. Stir in prawn mixture and bean sprouts, stir-fry until prawns are tender. Serve with rice, if desired.

Hot Spicy Pesto: Blend or process all ingredients until smooth.

Serves 4.

- Pesto can be prepared a day ahead.
- Storage: Covered, in refrigerator.
- Freeze: Not suitable.
- Microwave: Not suitable.

FISH PACKETS WITH CHIVE BUTTER

60g butter, softened
1 tablespoon lemon juice
1 tablespoon chopped fresh chives
1 tablespoon mayonnaise
1 medium (about 120g) carrot
1 medium (about 100g) zucchini
4 white fish fillets

Combine butter, juice, chives and mayonnaise in bowl; mix well.

Using vegetable peeler, peel thin strips lengthways from carrot and zucchini. Place vegetables on 4 large pieces of foil, top with fish and butter mixture; seal foil to make a packet. Grill, barbecue or bake packets in hot oven about 10 minutes or until fish is tender. Serve with salad or vegetables, if desired.

Serves 4.

- Recipe best made just before serving.
- Freeze: Not suitable.
- Microwave: Not suitable.

SALMON LOAVES WITH LEMON DILL SAUCE

440g can salmon
1½ cups cooked white rice
2 eggs, lightly beaten
2 green shallots, chopped
1 tablespoon lemon juice
½ cup grated parmesan cheese
3 large spinach (silverbeet) leaves, shredded
1 tablespoon stale breadcrumbs

LEMON DILL SAUCE
30g butter
½ cup water
2 teaspoons cornflour
2 tablespoons lemon juice
½ teaspoon dried dill tips

Lightly grease 4 x 5½cm x 10cm loaf tins. Drain and flake salmon, reserve salmon juice for sauce. Combine salmon, rice, eggs, shallots, lemon juice, cheese and spinach in bowl; mix well. Press salmon mixture into prepared tins, sprinkle with breadcrumbs.

Bake, uncovered, in moderately hot oven about 20 minutes or until firm. Stand 5 minutes before removing from tins. Serve loaves with lemon dill sauce. Serve with vegetables, if desired.

Lemon Dill Sauce: Combine butter, water, blended cornflour and juice with reserved salmon juice in pan, stir over heat until mixture boils and thickens; stir in dill; mix well.

Serves 4.

- Recipe can be prepared a day ahead.
- Storage: Covered, in refrigerator.
- Freeze: Suitable.
- Microwave: Sauce suitable.

LEFT: From top: Fish Packets with Chive Butter, Prawns with Hot Spicy Pesto.
RIGHT: Salmon Loaves with Lemon Dill Sauce.

Left: Woven basketware from Corso de Fiori
Right: China from Johnson Bros

SMOKED FISH RISOTTO

600g smoked fish
40g butter
1 tablespoon oil
6 green shallots, sliced
1 teaspoon dried oregano leaves
1½ cups long-grain rice
3 cups boiling water
1 large chicken stock cube, crumbled
1 cup (125g) frozen peas, thawed

Cook fish in pan of simmering water about 5 minutes or until tender. Drain fish, flake with fork.

Heat butter and oil in large pan, add shallots and oregano, cook, stirring, until shallots are tender. Stir in rice, water and stock cube, bring to boil, simmer, covered, about 10 minutes or until rice is tender and liquid absorbed; stir occasionally during cooking. Stir in fish and peas, stir until heated through.

Serves 4.

■ Recipe best made just before serving.
■ Freeze: Not suitable.
■ Microwave: Suitable.

CURRIED PRAWNS WITH PASTRY TRIANGLES

1 sheet ready-rolled puff pastry
1 egg yolk
1 medium (about 120g) carrot
1 medium (about 100g) zucchini
1 tablespoon oil
2 teaspoons curry powder
3 green shallots, sliced
2 teaspoons light soy sauce
500g cooked shelled prawns
2 teaspoons cornflour
¾ cup water
1 small chicken stock cube, crumbled

Brush pastry with egg yolk, run fork over surface to make decorative lines. Cut pastry into quarters, then each quarter in half to form 8 triangles. Place triangles on oven tray, bake in moderately hot oven about 8 minutes or until browned.

Meanwhile, cut carrot and zucchini into thin strips. Heat oil in pan, add curry powder, cook, stirring, 1 minute. Add carrot, zucchini and shallots, cook, stirring, until vegetables are just tender. Stir in sauce, prawns and blended cornflour and water, and stock cube; stir over heat until mixture boils and thickens. Serve pastry triangles with curried prawns.

Serves 4.

■ Recipe best made just before serving.
■ Freeze: Not suitable.
■ Microwave: Curried prawns suitable.

PEPPERS WITH SALMON AND PASTA

2 large red peppers
4 green shallots, chopped
1 cup cooked risoni pasta or rice
440g can salmon, drained, flaked
¼ cup cream
2 teaspoons seeded mustard
½ cup grated tasty cheese
¼ cup grated parmesan cheese

Cut peppers in half lengthways, remove seeds and membranes. Boil, steam or microwave peppers until just tender, rinse under cold water; drain.

Reserve 2 teaspoons shallots for topping. Combine pasta, salmon, remaining shallots, cream, mustard and tasty cheese in bowl. Divide salmon mixture evenly between peppers; sprinkle with parmesan cheese.

Place peppers on oven tray, bake, uncovered, in hot oven about 7 minutes or until filling is hot and cheese browned. Serve sprinkled with reserved shallots. Serve with salad, if desired.

Serves 4.

■ Recipe best made just before serving.
■ Freeze: Not suitable.
■ Microwave: Peppers suitable.

LEFT: Clockwise from top left: Smoked Fish Risotto, Peppers with Salmon and Pasta, Curried Prawns with Pastry Triangles.

Pottery urn and fish from Corso de Fiori

SPAGHETTI WITH TOMATO AND ANCHOVY SAUCE

500g spaghetti pasta
1 tablespoon oil
2 red peppers, sliced
2 yellow peppers, sliced
5 green shallots, sliced
2 x 410g cans tomatoes
2 x 56g cans anchovy fillets,
**   drained, chopped**
2 tablespoons chopped fresh chives
2 tablespoons chopped fresh parsley

Add pasta to large pan of boiling water, boil, uncovered, until just tender; drain.

Meanwhile, heat oil in pan, add peppers, cook, stirring, 1 minute. Add shallots, undrained crushed tomatoes, anchovies and herbs; bring to boil, simmer, uncovered, 8 minutes. Serve sauce over pasta. Serve with salad, if desired.

Serves 4.

■ Sauce can be prepared a day ahead.
■ Storage: Covered, in refrigerator.
■ Freeze: Not suitable.
■ Microwave: Suitable.

GRILLED SALMON CUTLETS WITH LIME BUTTER

4 salmon cutlets

MARINADE
1 teaspoon grated lime rind
1 tablespoon lime juice
1 tablespoon oil
½ teaspoon dried dill tips
¼ teaspoon dried chilli flakes

LIME BUTTER
90g butter, softened
1 teaspoon grated lime rind
½ teaspoon dried dill tips

Pour marinade over salmon in bowl, cover, refrigerate 3 hours or overnight.

Grill or barbecue salmon until tender. Serve with lime butter. Serve with salad or vegetables, if desired.
Marinade: Combine all ingredients in bowl; mix well.
Lime Butter: Beat butter in small bowl until creamy; beat in rind and dill. Shape butter into log, wrap in foil, freeze until firm.

Serves 4.

■ Recipe can be prepared a day ahead.
■ Storage: Covered, in refrigerator.
■ Freeze: Butter suitable.
■ Microwave: Not suitable.

SEAFOOD RISOTTO

30g butter
500g marinara mix
1 tablespoon olive oil
1 clove garlic, crushed
200g mushrooms, chopped
100g snow peas, sliced
4 green shallots, chopped
4 slices (about 75g) smoked
**   salmon, chopped**
4 cups cooked rice
2 tablespoons chopped fresh parsley
¼ cup lemon juice
¼ cup grated parmesan cheese

Heat butter in pan, add marinara mix, cook, stirring, until tender, remove marinara mix from pan. Heat oil in pan, add garlic, mushrooms and peas, cook, stirring, until peas are tender. Add marinara mix, shallots, salmon, rice, parsley and juice, stir until heated through. Sprinkle with cheese.

Serves 4.

■ Recipe best made just before serving.
■ Freeze: Not suitable.
■ Microwave: Suitable.

SMOKED SALMON AND SPINACH PIZZAS

½ cup tomato pasta sauce
4 pitta pocket breads
1 cup (125g) grated tasty cheese
¼ bunch (10 leaves) English spinach,
**   shredded**
100g smoked salmon pieces
1 small onion, sliced
2 teaspoons drained capers
1 cup (125g) grated tasty
**   cheese, extra**
½ teaspoon dried dill tips
¼ cup sour cream

Spread sauce evenly over pitta breads, place breads on oven tray. Sprinkle breads with cheese, spinach, salmon, onion and capers; sprinkle with extra cheese and dill. Bake in moderate oven about 12 minutes or until heated through. Top with teaspoons of sour cream, return to oven about 1 minute or until cream is warm. Serve with salad, if desired.

Serves 4.

■ Recipe best made just before serving.
■ Freeze: Not suitable.
■ Microwave: Not suitable.

LEFT: Clockwise from top left: Seafood Risotto, Grilled Salmon Cutlets with Lime Butter, Spaghetti with Tomato and Anchovy Sauce.
RIGHT: Smoked Salmon and Spinach Pizzas.

Plates from Incorporated Agencies

❖ HONEYED FISH KEBABS

500g white fish fillets
12 baby yellow squash
12 cherry tomatoes
12 baby mushrooms

MARINADE
2 tablespoons light soy sauce
1 tablespoon honey
1 clove garlic, crushed
1 tablespoon sweet sherry
1 tablespoon lemon juice

Cut fish into 2cm cubes. Combine fish and marinade in bowl, cover, refrigerate several hours or overnight.

Drain fish from marinade, reserve marinade. Boil, steam or microwave squash until just tender; drain. Thread fish, squash, tomatoes and mushrooms onto 12 skewers. Grill or barbecue kebabs until lightly browned and cooked through, brushing occasionally with reserved marinade. Serve kebabs with rice or salad, if desired.
Marinade: Combine all ingredients in bowl; mix well.
Serves 4.
- Recipe can be prepared a day ahead.
- Storage: Covered, in refrigerator.
- Freeze: Not suitable.
- Microwave: Squash suitable.

FISH WITH GINGERED PINEAPPLE SAUCE

4 white fish fillets

GINGERED PINEAPPLE SAUCE
1 small pineapple, peeled
60g butter
2 teaspoons finely chopped fresh ginger
1 tablespoon sugar
1½ tablespoons light soy sauce
1½ teaspoons cornflour
½ cup water
2 tablespoons chopped fresh chives

Poach or microwave fish until cooked through. Serve with gingered pineapple

sauce. Serve with salad or rice, if desired.
Gingered Pineapple Sauce: Cut pineapple into quarters lengthways, remove and discard core; slice pineapple. Heat butter in pan, add pineapple and ginger, cook, stirring, 1 minute. Add sugar, sauce and blended cornflour and water. Stir over heat until mixture boils and thickens; add chives; mix well.

Serves 4.

- Gingered pineapple sauce can be made 2 days ahead, add chives just before serving.
- Storage: Covered, in refrigerator.
- Freeze: Not suitable.
- Microwave: Suitable.

FISH WITH OLIVE AND ANCHOVY SAUCE

¼ cup olive oil
1 onion, chopped
2 cloves garlic, crushed
1 teaspoon sambal oelek
410g can tomatoes
¼ cup dry red wine
½ cup black olives
45g can anchovy fillets,
    drained, chopped
1 tablespoon drained capers
1 teaspoon sugar
1 teaspoon cracked black
    peppercorns
4 white fish cutlets

Heat oil in pan, add onion and garlic, cook, stirring, until onion is soft. Stir in sambal oelek, undrained crushed tomatoes and wine, bring to boil, simmer, uncovered, about 2 minutes or until slightly thickened. Stir in olives, anchovies, capers, sugar and peppercorns; stir until hot.

Meanwhile, grill or barbecue fish until tender. Serve sauce over fish. Serve with salad or vegetables, if desired.

Serves 4.

- Recipe best made just before serving.
- Freeze: Not suitable.
- Microwave: Sauce suitable.

LEFT: From left: Honeyed Fish Kebabs, Fish with Gingered Pineapple Sauce.
ABOVE: Fish with Olive and Anchovy Sauce.

Left: Serving ware from Incorporated Agencies
Above: Plate from Clay Things

TROUT WITH CREAMY SUN-DRIED TOMATO SAUCE

4 rainbow trout
30g butter, melted
1 clove garlic, crushed
½ cup drained sun-dried
   tomatoes, sliced
⅔ cup thickened cream
1 tablespoon lime juice
1 teaspoon cornflour
¼ cup water

Place trout in single layer in greased ovenproof dish, brush with butter. Bake, uncovered, in moderate oven about 20 minutes or until tender.

Meanwhile, heat garlic and tomatoes in pan, stir in cream, juice and blended corn-flour and water, stir over heat until mixture boils and thickens. Serve sauce over fish. Serve with salad or vegetables, if desired.
Serves 4.

■ Sauce can be prepared a day ahead.
■ Storage: Covered, in refrigerator.
■ Freeze: Not suitable.
■ Microwave: Suitable.

SWEET AND SOUR FISH

2 tablespoons oil
4 white fish fillets, chopped
2 onions, chopped
2 teaspoons grated fresh ginger
200g mushrooms, chopped
1 large (about 180g) carrot, chopped
2 sticks celery, chopped
1 bunch (12 spears) fresh
   asparagus, chopped
425g can baby corn, drained
¼ cup sugar
¼ cup white vinegar
2 tablespoons light soy sauce
1 tablespoon tomato sauce
1 tablespoon cornflour
½ cup water

Heat oil in large pan or wok, add fish, stir-fry until lightly browned and tender, remove fish from pan.

Add onions and ginger to pan, stir-fry until onions are soft. Stir in mushrooms, carrot, celery, asparagus, corn, sugar, vinegar and sauces. Bring to boil, simmer, covered, until vegetables are just tender. Stir in blended cornflour and water, stir over heat until mixture boils and thickens; stir in fish. Serve with rice, if desired.
Serves 4.

■ Recipe best made just before serving.
■ Freeze: Not suitable.
■ Microwave: Not suitable.

BELOW: Trout with Creamy Sun-Dried Tomato Sauce.
RIGHT: From left: Sweet and Sour Fish, Salmon and Corn Tacos with Guacamole.

Below: Plate and cloth from Home and Garden; tiles from Country Floors. Right: Plate from Corso de Fiori

SALMON AND CORN TACOS WITH GUACAMOLE

440g can salmon, drained, flaked
½ cup corn kernels, drained
1 tablespoon chopped fresh parsley
¼ cup mayonnaise
6 lettuce leaves, shredded
1 large tomato, chopped
1½ cups (190g) grated tasty cheese
8 taco shells

GUACAMOLE
1 ripe avocado, chopped
1 clove garlic, crushed
1 tablespoon lime juice
few drops tabasco sauce
¼ cup sour cream

Combine salmon, corn, parsley and mayonnaise in bowl.

Divide lettuce, salmon mixture, tomato and cheese between taco shells; top with guacamole. Serve with salad, if desired.

Guacamole: Blend or process all ingredients until smooth.

Serves 4.

- Recipe can be prepared several hours ahead.
- Storage: Covered, in refrigerator.
- Freeze: Not suitable.

CITRUS FISH PARCELS

4 white fish cutlets
1 teaspoon dried thyme leaves
⅓ cup orange juice concentrate
3 green shallots, chopped
1 teaspoon lemon pepper

Place each cutlet onto a large piece of foil, sprinkle with thyme, juice, shallots and pepper, seal to make a parcel. Place parcels in single layer in ovenproof dish, bake in hot oven or barbecue about 15 minutes or until fish is tender. Serve with pasta, vegetables or salad, if desired.

Serves 4.

■ Recipe best made just before serving.
■ Freeze: Not suitable.
■ Microwave: Not suitable.

TUNA AND GREEN VEGETABLE SALAD

200g broccoli, chopped
100g green beans, chopped
100g snow peas
lettuce
425g can tuna, drained, flaked
1 onion, sliced
2 medium (about 200g) zucchini, sliced

DRESSING
½ cup oil
2 teaspoons grated lemon rind
¼ cup lemon juice
1 clove garlic, crushed
2 tablespoons chopped fresh chives

Add broccoli and beans to pan of boiling water, return to boil, boil 1 minute, add peas, drain immediately; rinse under cold water, drain well. Tear lettuce into large pieces. Combine all ingredients in bowl. Add dressing; mix gently.
Dressing: Combine all ingredients in jar; shake well.

Serves 4.

■ Recipe can be prepared 3 hours ahead.
■ Storage: Covered, in refrigerator.
■ Freeze: Not suitable.
■ Microwave: Vegetables suitable.

PASTA SHELLS WITH TUNA AND PIMIENTOS

300g pasta shells
¼ cup olive oil
1 onion, finely chopped
4 cloves garlic, crushed
410g can red pimientos, drained, sliced
425g can tuna, drained, flaked
1 cup water
¼ cup lemon juice
¼ cup shredded fresh basil

Add pasta to large pan of boiling water, boil, uncovered, until just tender; drain.
    Meanwhile, heat oil in large pan, add onion and garlic, cook, stirring, until onion is soft. Stir in pimientos, tuna, water and juice, bring to boil; remove from heat, stir in basil. Stir sauce through pasta.

Serves 4.

■ Recipe can be made a day ahead and served cold.
■ Storage: Covered, in refrigerator.
■ Freeze: Not suitable.
■ Microwave: Suitable.

SPAGHETTI WITH SEAFOOD AND HERBS

350g spaghetti pasta
1 large (about 180g) carrot, sliced
⅓ cup oil
500g uncooked shelled prawns
150g snow peas
500g scallops
2 cloves garlic, crushed
⅓ cup chopped fresh basil
2 tablespoons chopped fresh chives
2 teaspoons grated lemon rind
⅓ cup lemon juice
1 teaspoon cracked black peppercorns

Add pasta to large pan of boiling water, boil, uncovered, until just tender; drain.
    Meanwhile, cut carrot into thin strips.

Heat oil in large pan or wok, add prawns, carrot, peas, scallops and garlic, stir-fry until seafood is tender. Add herbs, rind, juice and pepper; stir until well combined. Toss seafood mixture through hot pasta. Serve with salad, if desired.

Serves 4.

■ Recipe best made just before serving.
■ Freeze: Not suitable.
■ Microwave: Suitable.

LEFT: Clockwise from top left: Pasta Shells with Tuna and Pimientos, Tuna and Green Vegetable Salad, Citrus Fish Parcels.
RIGHT: Spaghetti with Seafood and Herbs.

Left: China from J. D. Milner Right: Plate from Clay Things

PRAWN AND CABBAGE SALAD WITH MINTY DRESSING

1kg cooked king prawns
1/6 medium (about 250g)
    cabbage, shredded
1 cup (80g) shredded red cabbage
1 stick celery, sliced
1 small green cucumber, sliced
1 red pepper, sliced

DRESSING
1/4 cup olive oil
1/4 cup orange juice
2 tablespoons lemon juice
1½ teaspoons fish sauce
1/4 cup chopped fresh mint
2 teaspoons castor sugar

Shell and devein prawns, leaving tails intact. Combine all ingredients in large bowl; pour over dressing, toss gently.

Dressing: Combine all ingredients in jar; shake well.

Serves 4.

■ Recipe can be prepared several hours ahead.
■ Storage: Covered, in refrigerator.
■ Freeze: Not suitable.

HOT AND SPICY FISH CUTLETS

4 white fish cutlets
¼ cup oil

MARINADE
1 tablespoon paprika
2 teaspoons ground ginger
2 teaspoons seasoned pepper
1 teaspoon curry powder
¼ teaspoon chilli powder
¼ cup brown vinegar
¼ cup tomato paste
1 cup dry white wine
2 cloves garlic, crushed

Combine fish and marinade in bowl, cover, refrigerate 3 hours or overnight.

Remove fish from marinade, reserve marinade. Heat oil in pan, add fish, cook until tender. Heat reserved marinade in pan, bring to boil, simmer, uncovered, 1 minute; pour sauce over fish. Serve with rice, vegetables or salad, if desired.

Marinade: Combine all ingredients in bowl, mix well.

Serves 4.

- Recipe can be prepared a day ahead.
- Storage: Covered, in refrigerator.
- Freeze: Uncooked marinated fish suitable.
- Microwave: Not suitable.

STIR-FRIED SCALLOPS WITH HAZELNUTS

500g fresh scallops
2 teaspoons grated fresh ginger
1 clove garlic, crushed
1 tablespoon oil
1 onion, sliced
1 yellow pepper, sliced
200g snow peas
1 tablespoon oil, extra
1 teaspoon cornflour
1 tablespoon light soy sauce
2 tablespoons chopped roasted hazelnuts

Combine scallops, ginger and garlic in bowl. Heat oil in large pan or wok. Add onion, pepper and peas, stir-fry until just tender, remove from pan.

Heat extra oil in pan, add scallop mixture, stir-fry until cooked through. Return onion mixture to pan, stir in blended cornflour and sauce, stir over heat until mixture boils and thickens; stir in nuts. Serve with rice, if desired.

Serves 4.

- Recipe best made just before serving.
- Freeze: Not suitable.
- Microwave: Not suitable.

LEFT: From back: Prawn and Cabbage Salad with Minty Dressing, Hot and Spicy Fish Cutlets.

ABOVE: Stir-Fried Scallops with Hazelnuts.

Vegetarian

■ *We've used canned beans and peas for speed and convenience, but it is cheaper to use dried varieties if you allow extra time; simply soak them overnight and boil in fresh water until tender next day.* ■ *Quantities of rice and pasta can be cooked ready for use and frozen until you need them; thaw before using. Both thaw and reheat well in the microwave oven.* ■ *Most varieties of pasta are interchangeable, one can be substituted for another in our recipes.* ■ *Tofu can be a handy meal standby, too; we used firm tofu. To keep any unused portions, place in a bowl, cover with water and store in the refrigerator; the water should be changed every day.* ■ *Frozen vegetables are time-savers in several of these recipes, but you can easily substitute fresh vegetables if you allow extra time to cook them until just tender before adding as specified.*

RED ONION, CHEESE AND VEGETABLE FRITTATA

2 tablespoons oil
2 red Spanish onions, sliced
1 clove garlic, crushed
2 medium (about 200g) zucchini, chopped
250g mushrooms, sliced
1 tablespoon chopped fresh chives
2 tablespoons chopped fresh basil
1 teaspoon cracked black peppercorns
8 eggs, lightly beaten
250g mozzarella cheese, chopped
2 tablespoons oil, extra

Heat oil in pan, add onions and garlic, cook, stirring, until onions are soft. Stir in zucchini and mushrooms, cook, stirring, until vegetables are tender; stir in herbs and peppercorns. Combine vegetable mixture, eggs and cheese in bowl

Heat extra oil in large pan, add egg mixture, cook over low heat until base is lightly browned and top is almost set. Place pan under griller on high heat until top is set and lightly browned. Cut into wedges. Serve with salad, if desired.

Serves 4.

■ Recipe best made just before serving.
■ Freeze: Not suitable.
■ Microwave: Not suitable.

RED CABBAGE COLESLAW

⅙ small (about 250g) red cabbage, finely shredded
1 carrot, grated
1 onion, thinly sliced
1 red pepper, thinly sliced
1 green pepper, thinly sliced
310g can red kidney beans, rinsed, drained
1 cup (100g) walnuts or pecans
1 apple, chopped
½ cup sultanas
1 small mango, sliced

DRESSING
⅔ cup white vinegar
2 tablespoons sugar
2 teaspoons curry powder
1 teaspoon turmeric
½ cup oil

Combine all ingredients in large bowl; pour over dressing, mix well.
Dressing: Combine all ingredients in jar; shake well.

Serves 4.

■ Recipe can be made a day ahead.
■ Storage: Covered, in refrigerator.
■ Freeze: Not suitable.

RIGHT: From top: Red Onion, Cheese and Vegetable Frittata, Red Cabbage Coleslaw.

Tiles from Country Floors; tea-towel from Country Road

RATATOUILLE WITH CHEESY PESTO BREAD

2 tablespoons olive oil
2 onions, sliced
2 cloves garlic, crushed
4 medium (about 400g) zucchini, chopped
1 red pepper, chopped
1 green pepper, chopped
150g yellow squash, quartered
410g can tomatoes
1½ teaspoons sugar
½ cup grated parmesan cheese

PESTO BREAD
1 cup basil leaves, firmly packed
¼ cup pine nuts
1 clove garlic, crushed
½ cup olive oil
2 Lebanese bread rounds
150g feta cheese, crumbled
½ cup grated parmesan cheese

Heat oil in pan, add onions and garlic, cook, stirring until onions are soft. Add zucchini, peppers and squash, cook, stirring, until vegetables are just tender. Add undrained crushed tomatoes and sugar, bring to boil, simmer, covered, about 10 minutes or until slightly thickened. Sprinkle ratatouille with cheese, serve with pesto bread.

Pesto Bread: Blend or process basil, nuts, garlic and oil until smooth. Cut bread in quarters, spread inside pockets with basil mixture. Place on oven tray, sprinkle with cheeses, grill about 3 minutes or until parmesan cheese melts.

Serves 4.

- Ratatouille can be made a day ahead. Bread best made just before serving.
- Storage: Covered, in refrigerator.
- Freeze: Not suitable.
- Microwave: Ratatouille suitable.

HERBED TORTELLINI

500g cheese tortellini pasta
90g butter
1 tablespoon chopped fresh parsley
2 teaspoons dried oregano leaves
½ teaspoon cracked black peppercorns
⅔ cup grated parmesan cheese

Add pasta to large pan of boiling water, boil, uncovered, until just tender; drain.

Heat butter in pan, add pasta, herbs, peppercorns and half the cheese, stir until heated through and combined. Sprinkle with remaining cheese.

Serves 4.

- Recipe best made just before serving.
- Freeze: Not suitable.
- Microwave: Suitable.

STIR-FRIED VEGETABLES WITH CURRIED OMELETTE

2 onions
2 tablespoons oil
2 sticks celery, chopped
1 red pepper, chopped
1 large (about 180g) carrot, sliced
2 medium (about 200g) zucchini, sliced
150g snow peas
2 tablespoons light soy sauce
1 tablespoon hoi sin sauce
2 tablespoons plum sauce
1 tablespoon water

CURRIED OMELETTE
2 tablespoons oil
1 small onion, chopped
2 teaspoons curry powder
4 eggs, lightly beaten
1 tablespoon chopped fresh coriander

Cut onions into wedges. Heat oil in large pan or wok, add onions and celery, stir-fry until onions are just tender Stir in pepper, carrot, zucchini and snow peas, stir-fry until vegetables are just tender. Stir in sauces and water, cook until heated through. Serve vegetables with omelette.

Curried Omelette: Heat oil in pan, add onion and curry powder, cook, stirring, until onion is soft. Pour combined eggs and coriander into pan over onion mixture; cook until set and lightly browned underneath. Turn omelette over, cook until lightly browned on other side. Cut omelette into quarters.

Serves 4.

▪ Recipe best made just before serving.
▪ Freeze: Not suitable.
▪ Microwave: Not suitable.

LEFT: Ratatouille with Cheesy Pesto Bread.
RIGHT: From top: Stir-Fried Vegetables with Curried Omelette, Herbed Tortellini.

Left: Fabric from Les Olivades
Right: Plates from Clay Things

HEARTY VEGETABLE SOUP WITH PESTO

30g butter
1 medium (about 120g) carrot, chopped
1 medium (about 150g) potato, chopped
60g green beans, chopped
1 medium (about 100g) zucchini, chopped
1 onion, finely chopped
410g can tomatoes
2 tablespoons plain flour
2 tablespoons tomato paste
1 large vegetable stock cube, crumbled
3 cups water
¼ teaspoon dried thyme leaves
2 teaspoons sugar
310g can butter beans, rinsed, drained

PESTO
1 cup basil leaves, firmly packed
½ bunch (20 leaves) English spinach
½ cup grated parmesan cheese
½ cup pine nuts
5 cloves garlic, chopped
½ cup olive oil

Heat butter in large pan, add vegetables and undrained crushed tomatoes, cook, stirring, until onion is soft. Stir in blended flour and paste, then stock cube, water, thyme and sugar. Stir over heat until mixture boils and thickens, simmer, uncovered, until vegetables are soft and soup is slightly thickened; stir in beans. Serve soup topped with pesto.
Pesto: Blend or process basil, spinach, cheese, nuts and garlic until smooth. Add oil gradually in a thin stream while motor is operating, blend until combined.

Serves 4.

- Soup can be made a day ahead.
- Storage: Covered, in refrigerator.
- Freeze: Not suitable.
- Microwave: Suitable.

LEFT: Clockwise from right: Spinach Timbales with Leek and Tomato Sauce, Fettucine Stir-Fry, Hearty Vegetable Soup with Pesto.

Serving ware from Accoutrement; fabric from Les Olivades

SPINACH TIMBALES WITH LEEK AND TOMATO SAUCE

250g packet frozen spinach, thawed
2 eggs, lightly beaten
100g mushrooms, chopped
1 cup (200g) ricotta cheese
1 cup (80g) grated parmesan cheese
1 onion, chopped
2 tablespoons chopped fresh chives
¼ teaspoon cracked black peppercorns

LEEK AND TOMATO SAUCE
20g butter
2 large (about 600g) leeks, sliced
300g can Tomato Supreme
1 tablespoon chopped fresh chives

Lightly grease 4 holes of 6-hole Texas muffin pan or 4 lightly greased ovenproof moulds (¾ cup capacity).

Squeeze spinach to remove excess water. Combine all ingredients in bowl, spoon evenly into prepared pan, bake, uncovered, in hot oven about 20 minutes or until firm. Stand timbales in pan 5 minutes before turning out. Serve with leek and tomato sauce.
Leek and Tomato Sauce: Heat butter in pan, add leeks, cook, stirring, until leeks are soft. Add Tomato Supreme and chives, stir until heated through.

Serves 4.

- Recipe can be prepared 2 hours ahead.
- Storage: Covered, in refrigerator.
- Freeze: Not suitable.
- Microwave: Suitable.

FETTUCINE STIR-FRY

500g fettucine pasta
2 teaspoons oil
2 teaspoons sesame oil
1 onion, chopped
2 cloves garlic, sliced
1 red pepper, sliced
425g can baby corn, drained
½ cup drained straw mushrooms
½ bunch (about 8 leaves) bok choy, shredded
1 tablespoon hoi sin sauce
⅓ cup tomato paste
1 tablespoon sugar
1 tablespoon cornflour
1½ cups water

Add pasta to large pan of boiling water, boil, uncovered until just tender; drain.

Meanwhile, heat oils in large pan or wok, add onion, garlic and pepper, stir-fry until onion is just soft. Stir in corn, mushrooms and bok choy, stir-fry until hot. Stir in sauce, paste, sugar and blended cornflour and water, stir until mixture boils and thickens slightly.

Serves 4.

- Recipe best made just before serving.
- Freeze: Not suitable.
- Microwave: Pasta suitable.

PEANUTTY BIG BURGERS

1 cup (150g) unsalted roasted peanuts
439g can garbanzos (chick peas),
    drained
1 medium (about 120g) carrot, grated
2 tablespoons chopped fresh parsley
2 tablespoons packaged
    breadcrumbs
1 tablespoon chutney
1 egg, lightly beaten
2 tablespoons oil
lettuce leaves
1 tomato, sliced
4 buns, halved, toasted

Process peanuts, garbanzos, carrot,
parsley, breadcrumbs, chutney and egg
until well combined. Divide mixture into 4
portions, shape into patties.

Heat oil in pan, add patties, cook until
browned on both sides and heated
through. Place lettuce and tomato on
buns, top with patties.

Serves 4.

- Patties can be prepared a day ahead.
- Storage: Covered, in refrigerator.
- Freeze: Not suitable.
- Microwave: Not suitable.

SPICY CHICK PEAS WITH VEGETABLES AND YOGURT

2 tablespoons oil
1 onion, chopped
2 cloves garlic, crushed
½ teaspoon curry powder
½ teaspoon ground cinnamon
¼ teaspoon ground cardamom
½ teaspoon dried chilli flakes
1½ tablespoons plain flour
1 large vegetable stock cube,
    crumbled
1½ cups water
2 tablespoons brown sugar
1kg packet Chunky Homestyle
    Frozen Vegetables, thawed
2 x 425g cans garbanzos (chick
    peas), rinsed, drained
200g carton plain yogurt

Heat oil in large pan or wok, add onion and
garlic, cook, stirring, until onion is soft; add
spices, cook, stirring, until aromatic. Stir in
flour, stir over heat until mixture is dry and
grainy. Remove from heat, gradually stir in
combined stock cube, water and sugar,
stir over heat until mixture boils and thickens. Add vegetables and garbanzos, stir
until hot. Serve with yogurt.

Serves 4.

- Recipe can be prepared a day ahead.
- Storage: Covered, in refrigerator.
- Freeze: Suitable.
- Microwave: Suitable.

CHILLI BEANS WITH TOFU

1 tablespoon oil
375g packet firm tofu, drained, cubed
1 tablespoon oil, extra
1 onion, sliced
1 green pepper, chopped
432g can red kidney beans, drained
410g can tomatoes, drained, crushed
1 tablespoon chilli sauce
¼ cup tomato paste
2 tablespoons tomato sauce
¼ teaspoon chilli powder
½ cup water

Heat oil in large pan or wok, add tofu, stir-
fry until tofu is browned; drain on absorbent paper. Add extra oil to pan, add onion
and pepper, stir-fry until onion is soft.
Return tofu to pan, add remaining ingredients, stir-fry until well combined and
heated through. Serve with rice, if desired.

Serves 4.

- Recipe best made just before serving.
- Freeze: Not suitable.
- Microwave: Not suitable.

WARM SPAGHETTI SALAD WITH TOFU

250g wholemeal spaghetti pasta
1 tablespoon oil
375g packet firm tofu, drained, cubed
2 cloves garlic, crushed
3 teaspoons grated fresh ginger
4 yellow squash, quartered
1 red pepper, sliced
1 cup water
2 teaspoons cornflour
3 teaspoons black bean sauce
2 teaspoons sugar
2 teaspoons brown vinegar
1 bunch (40 leaves) English
    spinach, chopped
1 cup fresh basil leaves,
    lightly packed

Add pasta to large pan of boiling water, boil, uncovered, until just tender; drain.

Meanwhile, heat oil in large pan or wok, add tofu, stir-fry until lightly browned; remove tofu from pan. Add garlic, ginger, squash and pepper to pan, stir-fry until squash are tender. Stir in water, blended cornflour, sauce, sugar and vinegar, stir until mixture boils and thickens. Stir in pasta, tofu, spinach and basil.

Serves 4.

- Recipe can be made a day ahead and served cold.
- Storage: Covered, in refrigerator.
- Freeze: Not suitable.
- Microwave: Pasta suitable.

FAR LEFT: Peanutty Big Burgers, Chilli Beans with Tofu.
LEFT: Spicy Chick Peas with Vegetables and Yogurt, Warm Spaghetti Salad with Tofu.

Far left and left: Bowls and glass from Accoutrement; fabric from Les Olivades

HOT NOODLES WITH SPINACH AND TOFU

375g packet fresh egg noodles
375g packet firm tofu, drained
1/4 cup oil
3 teaspoons sesame oil
1 tablespoon grated fresh ginger
pinch ground saffron
1 bunch (40 leaves) English
    spinach, chopped
1 teaspoon cornflour
1/4 cup light soy sauce
1 tablespoon sambal oelek
1/4 cup lemon juice
300g (3 cups) bean sprouts

Cover noodles with boiling water in bowl, stand 1 minute; drain.

Cut tofu into 1cm cubes. Heat oil in large pan or wok, add tofu, stir-fry until lightly browned; drain on absorbent paper. Drain oil from pan. Add sesame oil to pan add ginger, saffron and spinach, stir-fry until spinach is just wilted. Add noodles, tofu, blended cornflour and sauce, sambal oelek, juice and sprouts to pan, stir-fry until mixture boils and thickens slightly.

Serves 4.

■ Recipe best made just before serving.
■ Freeze: Not suitable.
■ Microwave: Not suitable.

CHEESY VEGETABLE PASTRIES

1 1/2 cups frozen mixed
    vegetables, thawed
1 teaspoon cracked black
    peppercorns
100g mozzarella cheese, chopped
2 tablespoons sunflower seed kernels
130g can creamed corn
1 tablespoon chopped fresh chives
2 teaspoons seeded mustard
2 sheets ready-rolled puff pastry
1 egg, lightly beaten

Combine vegetables, peppercorns, cheese, seeds, corn, chives and mustard in bowl. Cut each pastry sheet in half, place on oven trays. Place quarter of the vegetable mixture in the centre of each piece of pastry, brush edges of pastry with egg. Fold pastry in half to enclose filling, press edges together with fork. Brush parcels with egg; cut 3 slits in top of each pastry parcel. Bake in hot oven about 10 minutes or until pastry is browned and filling heated through.

Serves 4.

■ Recipe best made just before serving.
■ Freeze: Suitable.
■ Microwave: Not suitable.

CHICK PEA AND RED ONION SALAD

439g can garbanzos (chick peas),
    rinsed, drained
4 green shallots, chopped
1 red Spanish onion, sliced
1 red pepper, sliced
2 tomatoes, chopped
lettuce

DRESSING
1 teaspoon dried oregano leaves
2 tablespoons lemon juice
1 tablespoon white wine vinegar
1/4 cup olive oil

Combine garbanzos, shallots, onion and pepper in bowl. Pour over dressing, cover, refrigerate 20 minutes. Add tomatoes and torn lettuce; mix well.
Dressing: Combine all ingredients in jar; shake well.

Serves 4.

■ Recipe can be prepared several hours ahead.
■ Storage: Covered, in refrigerator.
■ Freeze: Not suitable.

RIGHT: Clockwise from left: Hot Noodles with Spinach and Tofu, Chick Pea and Red Onion Salad, Cheesy Vegetable Pastries.

Plates from The Design Store; fabric from Les Olivades

RICE AND ZUCCHINI PATTIES

1½ cups cooked brown rice
3 medium (about 300g) zucchini,
** grated**
1 onion, chopped
1 tablespoon chopped fresh parsley
2 teaspoons seasoned pepper
2 eggs, lightly beaten
1 cup (70g) stale breadcrumbs
130g can creamed corn
¼ cup oil

Combine rice, zucchini, onion, parsley, pepper, eggs, breadcrumbs and corn in bowl; mix well. Divide mixture into 12 portions, shape into patties.

Heat oil in pan, add patties, cook until well browned and heated through, drain on absorbent paper. Serve with chutney and salad, if desired.

Serves 4.

- ■ Recipe best made just before serving.
- ■ Freeze: Cooked patties suitable.
- ■ Microwave: Not suitable.

CHUNKY VEGETABLE STIR-FRY IN BLACK BEAN SAUCE

375g packet Vege-Hot Dogs
1 tablespoon oil
⅔ cup roasted unsalted cashews
1 tablespoon oil, extra
100g green beans, sliced
2 medium (about 200g) zucchini,
** sliced**
200g broccoli, chopped
50g snow peas
1 red pepper, chopped
1 green pepper, chopped

BLACK BEAN SAUCE
¼ cup black bean sauce
½ cup water
2 teaspoons lime juice
2 teaspoons sugar

Cut Hot Dogs into 2cm pieces. Heat oil in large pan or wok, add cashews, stir-fry until lightly browned; drain on absorbent paper. Add extra oil to pan, add vegetables, stir-fry until vegetables are just tender. Add Hot Dog chunks, cashews and black bean sauce, stir over heat until well combined and heated through.
Black Bean Sauce: Combine all ingredients in bowl; mix well.

Serves 4.

- ■ Sauce can be made a day ahead.
- ■ Storage: Covered, in refrigerator.
- ■ Freeze: Not suitable.
- ■ Microwave: Suitable.

POTATO NUT CROQUETTES WITH TOMATO SAUCE

2 cups boiling water
⅔ cup packaged dry potato powder
½ bunch (20 leaves) English
** spinach, shredded**
2 green shallots, chopped
½ teaspoon dried thyme leaves
1 teaspoon caraway seeds, crushed
30g butter, softened
1 egg yolk
1 cup (150g) roasted hazelnuts,
** chopped**

TOMATO SAUCE
30g butter
1 onion, sliced
1 clove garlic, crushed
410g can tomatoes
1 teaspoon sugar
2 teaspoons tomato paste

Combine water and potato in bowl. Boil, steam or microwave spinach until just wilted, drain; squeeze to remove water. Combine potato mixture, spinach, shallots, thyme, seeds, butter and yolk in bowl, mix well.

Divide mixture into 8 portions, shape into croquettes, roll in nuts, pressing lightly to coat evenly. Place croquettes on greased oven tray, bake in hot oven about 10 minutes or until heated through. Serve with tomato sauce. Serve with salad or vegetables, if desired.
Tomato Sauce: Heat butter in pan, add onion and garlic, cook, stirring, until onion is soft. Add undrained crushed tomatoes, sugar and paste, bring to boil, simmer, uncovered, until thickened slightly.

Serves 4.

- ■ Recipe can be made 2 days ahead.
- ■ Storage: Covered, in refrigerator.
- ■ Freeze: Sauce suitable.
- ■ Microwave: Sauce suitable.

LEFT: From top: Chunky Vegetable Stir-Fry in Black Bean Sauce, Rice and Zucchini Patties. ABOVE: Potato Nut Croquettes with Tomato Sauce.

Above: Plate from Clay Things

POTATO AND ZUCCHINI FRITTATA

½ cup frozen peas
1 medium (about 150g) potato, sliced
1 tablespoon oil
1 tablespoon oil, extra
1 onion, chopped
1 red pepper, chopped
2 medium (about 200g) zucchini, grated
¼ cup black olives, chopped
2 tablespoons chopped fresh basil
8 eggs, lightly beaten
½ cup grated smoked cheese

Pour boiling water over peas, stand 1 minute, drain.

Cut potato into thin strips. Heat oil in pan, add potato, cook, stirring, until lightly browned; remove potato from pan. Heat extra oil in pan, add onion, pepper and zucchini, cook, stirring, until onion is soft; stir in peas, olives and basil.

Combine potato, vegetable mixture and eggs in bowl; mix well. Pour mixture into greased shallow pan, cook over low heat until browned underneath. Sprinkle with cheese, place pan under hot griller, grill until cheese is melted and frittata set. Serve with salad or vegetables, if desired.

Serves 4.

■ Recipe best made just before serving.
■ Freeze: Not suitable.
■ Microwave: Not suitable.

PASTA WITH SPINACH AND EGGPLANT SAUCE

400g shell pasta
½ cup olive oil
2 onions, sliced
6 (about 300g) baby eggplants, chopped
¼ cup pine nuts
2 cloves garlic, crushed
250g baby mushrooms, sliced
1 bunch (about 40 leaves) English spinach, shredded
250g mozzarella cheese, chopped
200g feta cheese, chopped

Add pasta to large pan of boiling water, boil, uncovered, until just tender; drain.

Meanwhile, heat oil in pan, add onions, eggplants, nuts and garlic, cook, stirring. until onion is soft. Stir in mushrooms and spinach, cook, stirring, until spinach is wilted. Combine spinach mixture with pasta in large bowl; add cheeses, toss gently to combine.

Serves 4.

■ Recipe best made just before serving.
■ Freeze: Not suitable.
■ Microwave: Suitable.

THICK VEGETABLE AND CORIANDER SOUP

50g butter
1 onion, finely chopped
1 medium leek, sliced
1 clove garlic, crushed
1 teaspoon ground cumin
1 parsnip, grated
½ white turnip, grated
2 medium (about 300g) potatoes, grated
1½ litres (6 cups) boiling water
2 large vegetable stock cubes, crumbled
½ cup cream
1 tablespoon chopped fresh coriander
1 tablespoon chopped fresh parsley
2 tablespoons cream, extra

Heat butter in large pan, add onion, leek and garlic, cook, stirring, until leek is soft; stir in cumin. Add remaining vegetables, water and stock cube to pan, bring to boil, boil, covered, about 10 minutes or until vegetables are soft. Blend or process vegetable mixture until smooth.

Return soup to pan, stir in cream and herbs. Serve with a swirl of extra cream. Serve with crusty bread, if desired.

Serves 4.

■ Recipe can be prepared a day ahead.
■ Storage: Covered, in refrigerator.
■ Freeze: Suitable.
■ Microwave: Suitable.

LEFT: Clockwise from right: Potato and Zucchini Frittata, Pasta with Spinach and Eggplant Sauce, Thick Vegetable and Coriander Soup.

Serving ware from Powder Blue; fabric from Les Olivades

TASTY EGGPLANT ROLLS

¼ cup olive oil
1 clove garlic, crushed
1 large (about 500g) eggplant, sliced
4 slices wholemeal Lebanese bread
⅓ cup hummus
2 onions, sliced
2 large (about 500g) tomatoes, sliced
⅓ cup chopped fresh
    flat-leafed parsley
2 teaspoons dried basil leaves
1 tablespoon chopped fresh mint
150g feta cheese, crumbled

Combine oil and garlic in bowl; reserve 2 teaspoons of the oil mixture. Brush eggplant with remaining oil mixture, grill until lightly browned.

Spread each slice of bread with hummus, top with some eggplant, onion, tomato, herbs and cheese. Roll bread around filling, secure with skewers, brush with reserved oil mixture.

Place rolls onto oven tray, bake, uncovered, in moderately hot oven about 10 minutes or until crisp and heated through.

Serves 4.

■ Can be prepared 3 hours ahead.
■ Storage: Covered, in refrigerator.
■ Freeze: Not suitable.
■ Microwave: Not suitable.

VEGETABLE AND RED LENTIL CURRY

40g butter
2 onions, sliced
1 tablespoon curry powder
1 teaspoon cumin seeds, crushed
2 tablespoons plain flour
150g can coconut cream
2¼ cups water
1 large vegetable stock cube,
    crumbled
1 cup (200g) red lentils
1kg packet frozen Chunky Home
    Style Vegetables

Heat butter in pan, add onions, cook, stirring, until onions are soft. Add curry powder and seeds, stir until fragrant. Stir in flour, stir over heat until mixture is dry and grainy. Remove from heat, gradually stir in cream, water and stock cube. Add lentils, bring to boil, simmer, uncovered, 8 minutes. Add vegetables, simmer, uncovered, 10 minutes or until lentils are soft.

Serves 4.

■ Recipe can be made 2 days ahead.
■ Storage: Covered, in refrigerator.
■ Freeze: Suitable.
■ Microwave: Suitable.

LEFT: From top: Vegetable and Red Lentil Curry, Tasty Eggplant Rolls.
ABOVE: Mushrooms with Cheesy Spinach Seasoning.

Left: Bowl from Clay Things. Above: Plates, jug and napkin from Accoutrement

MUSHROOMS WITH CHEESY SPINACH SEASONING

12 (about 500g) large flat mushrooms
40g butter
1 onion, finely chopped
2 cloves garlic, crushed
½ small red pepper, finely chopped
½ bunch (20 leaves) English spinach,
    finely shredded
1 tablespoon chopped fresh basil
1 teaspoon dried tarragon leaves
150g feta cheese, crumbled
1½ cups (100g) stale breadcrumbs

TOMATO SAUCE
3 teaspoons cornflour
1½ cups water
⅓ cup tomato paste

Discard stems from mushrooms. Heat butter in pan, add onion and garlic, cook, stirring, until onion is soft. Add pepper, spinach, basil and tarragon, cook, stirring, until pepper is tender. Combine vegetable mixture, cheese and breadcrumbs in bowl; mix well.

Place mushrooms on oven tray, top with vegetable mixture, bake, uncovered, in moderate oven about 10 minutes or until heated through. Serve mushrooms with tomato sauce.

Tomato Sauce: Blend cornflour with a little of the water in pan, stir in remaining water and paste. Stir over heat until mixture boils and thickens.

Serves 4.

■ Spinach seasoning and tomato sauce can be prepared a day ahead.
■ Storage: Covered, in refrigerator.
■ Freeze: Not suitable.
■ Microwave: Suitable.

NUTTY PASTA WITH PUMPKIN AND CAULIFLOWER

400g pumpkin
200g penne pasta
300g cauliflower, chopped
40g butter
2 onions, sliced
½ cup pine nuts

TOMATO BASIL DRESSING
½ cup olive oil
¼ cup white wine vinegar
1 teaspoon castor sugar
1 green shallot, chopped
1 tomato, peeled, seeded, chopped
½ cup shredded fresh basil

Cut pumpkin into 2cm cubes. Add pasta to large pan of boiling water, boil, uncovered, until almost tender. Add pumpkin and cauliflower, cook until vegetables are just tender; drain.

Meanwhile, heat butter in pan, add onions, cook, stirring, until onions are browned. Add nuts, cook, stirring, until nuts are lightly browned. Combine pasta mixture, onion mixture and tomato basil dressing in bowl.

Tomato Basil Dressing: Combine all ingredients in bowl; mix well

Serves 4.

- Recipe can be made a day ahead.
- Storage: Covered, in refrigerator.
- Freeze: Not suitable.
- Microwave: Suitable.

BELOW: Nutty Pasta with Pumpkin and Cauliflower.

Fabric from Les Olivades

PANTRY CHECK LIST

Here, we've listed basic ingredients used many times in our recipes; if you have a selection on hand, it makes preparing these meals even easier. All you will then need to buy is fresh foods such as meat, poultry, seafood, fruit and vegetables, etc, before you start to cook, or have a selection in your freezer.

ALCOHOL
brandy
dry red wine
dry white wine
green ginger wine
marsala
sherry (dry and sweet)
tawny port

BREADCRUMBS
packaged

CANNED PRODUCTS
Savoury
anchovy fillets
artichoke hearts
baby carrots
baked beans
bamboo shoots
butter beans
coconut cream
coconut milk
corn (baby, creamed, kernels)
crab
garbanzos (chick peas)
Mushroom Supreme
potatoes
red kidney beans
red pimientos
salmon
straw mushrooms
tomatoes
Tomato Supreme
tuna
Sweet
apricot halves in syrup
blueberries in syrup
lychees in syrup
mangoes in syrup
pear halves in syrup
pineapple pieces in syrup

CONDIMENTS AND FLAVOURINGS
capers
celery salt
chutney (fruit and mango)
garlic
garlic salt
gherkins
green peppercorns
horseradish cream
jelly (mint, redcurrant)
lemon pepper seasoning
mayonnaise
mustard (French and seeded)
peanut butter
red lumpfish roe
sambal oelek
stock cubes (chicken, beef and vegetable)
tomato paste
tomato puree
tomato sauce
sun-dried tomatoes
vindaloo curry paste

EGGS: 60g

DAIRY PRODUCE
Butter
salted and unsalted
Cheese
cream cheese
mozzarella
parmesan
tasty

CREAM
fresh
sour
thickened

FLOUR
arrowroot
cornflour
plain flour
self-raising flour

FROZEN PRODUCTS
mixed vegetables
peas
spinach

FRUIT, dried
apricots
pears
raisins
sultanas

HERBS, dried
dill
marjoram
mixed
oregano
rosemary
tarragon
thyme

JAM, etc
honey
marmalade

JUICES
apple
apricot nectar
orange

NUTS
almonds (flaked, ground, slivered)
cashews
hazelnuts
pecans
pine nuts
pistachios
unsalted peanuts
walnuts

OIL
olive
polyunsaturated
sesame

OLIVES
black
green pimiento-stuffed
olive paste

PASTA, dried
fettucine
lasagne
penne
risoni
shells
spaghetti (plain and wholemeal)
tortellini

PASTRY, etc
ready-rolled puff pastry
taco shells
vol-au-vent cases

RICE AND PULSES
black beans, packaged
lentils
rice (white, brown, long-grain, short-grain)

SAUCES
barbecue
black bean
chilli
fish
hoi sin
oyster
plum
soy (light and dark)
sweet and sour
tabasco
teryaki
tomato
Worcestershire

SPICES
allspice
caraway seeds
cardamom
chilli flakes
chilli powder
cinnamon
coriander (ground)
cumin seeds
curry powder
five spice powder
garam masala
ginger (ground)
mixed spice
nutmeg
paprika
saffron (ground and threads)
seasoned pepper
turmeric

SUGAR
brown
castor
crystal

TOMATO
canned whole tomatoes
tomato paste
puree
sauce
sun-dried tomatoes
Tomato Supreme

VINEGAR
balsamic
brown
red wine
tarragon
white
white wine

SPEEDY SHORT CUTS

Fuss-free ideas like these can save heaps of cooking time when you're making any of our recipes.

■ Steaming vegetables is faster than boiling, or you can microwave vegetables and potatoes in their jackets for fast accompaniments.

■ Use frozen, canned or dehydrated vegetables when fresh are not in season.

■ Cook rice and pasta ahead; they keep well, covered, in the refrigerator for a few days, or in the freezer for 4 months. They thaw and reheat quickly in the microwave oven.

■ Make dressings ahead where possible, cover and store in the refrigerator.

■ For fast flavour, we've used dried herbs, spices, bottled sauces, different vegetable salts and seasoned peppers.

■ For convenience, we've used more dried herbs than we normally do but you can substitute fresh herbs, if you prefer. Use in the proportion of 1:4 for fresh herbs; for example, 1 teaspoon dried herbs equals 4 teaspoons (1 tablespoon) chopped fresh herbs.

■ Chop fresh herbs, place in ice trays, fill trays with water and freeze; use cubes as required. They keep for about 2 months.

■ Whole chillies freeze well, as do grated rinds.

■ Use packaged parmesan cheese for convenience although fresh parmesan cheese can be bought already grated; keep, covered, in the refrigerator.

■ Use packaged breadcrumbs or make your own by grating, blending and processing stale bread; store, covered, in the refrigerator for a few days, or freeze for several months.

EQUIPMENT - keep it simple

■ Simple equipment is all you need. Have sharp knives, a large chopping board, a durable work bench, saucepans, wok or frypan, metric measuring cups and spoons, kitchen scales, mixing bowls and plates, spoons, heatproof tongs and forks, vegetable peeler and any other favourite items.

MICROWAVING

■ We've suggested you use the microwave oven with more leniency than we usually do as it's such a great speed aid; however, in some cases the food will not look like our pictures nor as it would if cooked in a conventional oven.

■ A browning plate, used as directed by the manufacturer, gives good colour, and can be used instead of pan-frying.

■ Always use microwave-proof cookware, and take extra care if microwaving ingredients such as fats, oil or sugar as some plastics cannot withstand the heat that can occur with these ingredients. Check the label of the cookware if in doubt, or contact the manufacturer.

Cup and Spoon Measurements

To ensure accuracy in your recipes use the standard metric measuring equipment approved by Standards Australia:
(a) 250 millilitre cup for measuring liquids. A litre jug *(capacity 4 cups)* is also available.
(b) a graduated set of four cups – measuring 1 cup, half, third and quarter cup – for items such as flour, sugar, etc. When measuring in these fractional cups, level off at the brim.
(c) a graduated set of four spoons: tablespoon *(20 millilitre liquid capacity)*, teaspoon *(5 millilitre)*, half and quarter teaspoons. The Australian, British and American teaspoon each has 5ml capacity.

Approximate cup and spoon conversion chart

Australian	American & British
1 cup	1¼ cups
¾ cup	1 cup
⅔ cup	¾ cup
½ cup	⅔ cup
⅓ cup	½ cup
¼ cup	⅓ cup
2 tablespoons	¼ cup
1 tablespoon	3 teaspoons

**All spoon measurements are level.
Note: NZ, USA and UK all use 15ml tablespoons.**

Oven Temperatures

Electric	C˙	F˙
Very slow	120	250
Slow	150	300
Moderately slow	160-180	325-350
Moderate	180-200	375-400
Moderately hot	210-230	425-450
Hot	240-250	475-500
Very hot	260	525-550

Gas	C˙	F˙
Very slow	120	250
Slow	150	300
Moderately slow	160	325
Moderate	180	350
Moderately hot	160	375
Hot	200	400
Very hot	230	450

We have used large eggs with an average weight of 60g each in all recipes.

Glossary

Here are some terms, names and alternatives to help everyone use and understand our recipes perfectly.

ALCOHOL: is optional but gives special flavour. You can use fruit juice, water or stock to make up the liquid content of our recipes.

ALMONDS:
Flaked: sliced almonds.
Ground: we used packaged, commercially ground nuts unless otherwise specified.
Slivered: almonds cut lengthways.

ARROWROOT: used mostly for thickening. Cornflour can be used instead.

BACON RASHERS: bacon slices.

BEAN SPROUTS: we used alfalfa sprouts and mung bean sprouts; either can be used.

BEEF:
Eye-fillet: tenderloin.
Minced beef: ground beef.
New York-style steak: a thick-cut steak from the sirloin.
Rib-eye: scotch fillet.
Round steak: boneless piece of meat from the front of the butt.
Rump steak: boneless piece of meat that covers the hip bone.
Scotch fillet: rib-eye.
Sirloin: piece of meat between the rump and the ribs; without bone.
T-bone: sirloin steak with the bone in and fillet eye attached; also known as porterhouse.

BEETROOT: regular round beet.

BLACK BEANS, SALTED PACKAGED: are fermented, salted soy beans. Canned and dried black beans can be substituted. Drain and rinse canned variety, soak and rinse dried variety. Leftover beans will keep for months in an airtight container in the refrigerator. Mash beans when cooking to release flavour.

BLACK BEAN SAUCE: made from fermented whole and crushed soy beans, water and wheat flour.

BREADCRUMBS:
Packaged: use fine packaged breadcrumbs.
Stale: use 1 or 2 day old white bread made into crumbs by grating, blending or processing.

BUTTER: use salted or unsalted (also called sweet) butter; 125g is equal to 1 stick butter.

CABANOSSI: a type of sausage; also known as cabana.

CALABRESE SALAMI: hot, spicy salami; includes chilli, red peppers, red wine and other spices.

CHEESE:
Bocconcini: small balls of mild delicate cheese packaged in water or whey to keep them white and soft.
Cottage: we used low-fat cottage cheese.
Cream cheese: also known as Philly.
Cream cheese spread: a spread made from cream and cheese; found in jars in the supermarket.
Fresh goats' milk: chevre; is fresh unripened cheese made from goats' milk.
Mozzarella: a fresh, semi-soft cheese with a delicate, clean, fresh curd taste; has a low melting point and stringy texture when heated.
Parmesan: sharp-tasting cheese used as a flavour accent.
Provolone: a mild cheese when young, similar to mozzarella. Golden yellow in colour, with a smooth shiny skin.
Ricotta: a fresh, unripened light curd cheese with a rich flavour.
Smoked: we used a firm smoked cheese.
Soft blue vein: soft, creamy, sweet cheese with delicate blue veining.
Tasty: use a firm good-tasting cheddar.

CHILLIES: are available in many different types and sizes. The small ones (birds' eye or bird peppers) are the hottest. Use tight rubber gloves when chopping fresh chillies as they can burn your skin. The seeds are the hottest part of the chillies so remove them if you want to reduce the heat content of recipes.
Flakes, dried: available at Asian food stores.
Powder: the Asian variety is the hottest and is made from ground chillies. It can be used as a substitute for fresh chillies in the proportion of ½ teaspoon ground chilli powder to 1 medium chopped fresh chilli.

COCONUT: we used desiccated coconut unless otherwise specified.
Shredded: thin strips of dried coconut.

COCONUT CREAM: available in cans and cartons in supermarkets and Asian stores; coconut milk can be substituted, although it is not as thick.

COCONUT MILK: available in cans from supermarkets.

CORIANDER: also known as cilantro and Chinese parsley, is essential to many south-east Asian cuisines; its seeds are the main ingredient of curry powder. A strongly flavoured herb, use it sparingly until you are accustomed to the unique flavor. Available fresh, ground and in seed form.

CORNFLOUR: cornstarch.

CORNMEAL: ground corn (maize); is similar to polenta but pale yellow in colour and finer.

One can be substituted for the other but results will be slightly different.
CREAM: a light pouring cream, also known as half 'n' half.
Sour: a thick commercially cultured soured cream.
Thickened (whipping): is specified when necessary in recipes. Double cream or cream with more than 35% fat can be substituted.

CURRY POWDER: a convenient combination of spices in powdered form. It consists of chilli, coriander, cumin, fennel, fenugreek and turmeric in varying proportions.

EGGPLANT: aubergine.

FENNEL, BULB: is eaten uncooked in salads or may be braised, steamed or stir-fried in savoury dishes.

FISH SAUCE: an essential ingredient in the cooking of a number of South East Asian countries, including Thailand and Vietnam. It is made from the liquid drained from salted, fermented anchovies. It has a very strong smell and taste. Use sparingly until you acquire the taste.

FIVE SPICE POWDER: a pungent mixture of ground spices which includes cinnamon, cloves, fennel, star anise and Szechwan peppers.

FLOUR, PLAIN: all-purpose flour.

GARAM MASALA: varied combinations of cardamom, cinnamon, cloves, coriander, cumin and nutmeg make this spice which is often used in Indian cooking. Sometimes pepper is used to make a hot variation.

GARBANZOS: canned chick peas.

GARLIC: can be used crushed, sliced or whole cloves; a bulb contains many cloves.

GARLIC SALT: mixture of fine garlic powder and free-running table salt.

GHERKIN: cornichon.

GINGER:
Fresh, green or root ginger: scrape away outside skin; grate, chop or slice ginger as required. Fresh, peeled ginger can be preserved with enough dry sherry to cover; keep in jar in refrigerator; it will keep for months.
Ground: is also available but should not be substituted for fresh ginger in any recipe.

GREEN GINGER WINE: an Australian-made alcoholic sweet wine infused with finely ground ginger.

GREEN PEPPERCORNS: in brine; available in cans or jars.

GREEN SHALLOTS: also known as scallions and spring onions. Do not confuse with the small golden shallots.

HERBS: we have specified when to use fresh or dried herbs. We used dried (not ground) herbs in the proportion of 1:4 for fresh herbs; e.g, 1 teaspoon dried herbs instead of 4 teaspoons (1 tablespoon) chopped fresh herbs.

HOI SIN SAUCE: is a thick sweet Chinese barbecue sauce made from a mixture of salted black beans, onion and garlic.

HORSERADISH CREAM: paste of horseradish, oil, mustard and flavourings.

HUMMUS: a paste of chick peas, tahini, garlic, lemon juice and olive oil.

KUMARA: orange-coloured sweet potato.

LEEK: a member of the onion family, resembles the green shallot but is larger.

125

LETTUCE: we used mostly cos, endive, mignonette, radicchio and red coral.

LUMPFISH ROE, RED: red eggs of the Arctic lumpfish. Has a pleasant fishy flavour.

MARINARA MIX: a mixture of uncooked, chopped seafood.

MARSALA: a sweet fortified wine.

MIXED SPICE: a blend of ground spices usually consisting of cinnamon, allspice and nutmeg.

MUSHROOMS:

Baby: small unopened mushrooms with a delicate flavour.

Chinese dried: unique in flavour; place mushrooms in bowl, cover with boiling water, stand 20 minutes. Drain mushrooms, discard stems, use caps as indicated in recipes.

Flat: large, soft, flat mushrooms with a rich strong flavour.

Straw: cultivated Chinese mushroom about the size and shape of a quail egg, cream at the base and grey-black on top. Flavour is earthy. Sold canned in water.

MUSHROOM SUPREME: canned baby mushrooms with milk, cream, cheese, onions and bacon.

MUSTARD:

Dry: available in powder form.

Seeded: a French style of mustard with crushed mustard seeds.

NOODLES:

Egg noodles, fresh: made from wheat flour and eggs, varying in thickness from fine strands to pieces as thick as a shoelace.

2 Minute, beef flavour: quick cook noodles with flavour sachet.

OIL: polyunsaturated vegetable oil.

OLIVE OIL: virgin oil is obtained only from the pulp of high-grade fruit. Pure olive oil is pressed from the pulp and kernels of second grade olives. Extra virgin olive oil is the purest quality virgin oil.

OLIVE PASTE: a paste of olives, olive oil, salt, vinegar and herbs.

OYSTER SAUCE: a rich brown sauce made from oysters cooked in salt and soy sauce, then thickened with different starches.

PARSLEY, FLAT-LEAFED: also known as continental parsley or Italian parsley.

PASTA SAUCE, BOTTLED: prepared sauce available from supermarkets.

PEPPERONI: a type of sausage made from ground pork and beef with added fat. Flavoured with ground red pepper.

PEPPERS: capsicum or bell peppers.

PIMIENTOS: canned or bottled peppers.

PITTA POCKET BREAD: 2-layered flat bread; can be cut open to form a pocket.

PLUM SAUCE: a dipping sauce which consists of plums preserved in vinegar, sweetened with sugar and flavoured with chillies and spices.

POLENTA: usually made from ground corn (maize); similar to cornmeal but coarser and darker in colour. One can be substituted for the other but results will be slightly different.

PORK:

American-style spare ribs: pork rib bones.

Butterfly: skinless, boneless mid-loin chop which has been split in half and flattened.

Fillet: skinless, boneless eye-fillet cut from the loin.

Steak: schnitzel, is usually cut from the leg or rump.

PRAWNS: also known as shrimp.

PROSCIUTTO: uncooked, unsmoked ham cured in salt; ready to eat when bought.

PRUNES: whole dried plums with a dark, wrinkled appearance.

PUFF PASTRY, READY-ROLLED: frozen sheets of puff pastry available from supermarkets.

RED SPANISH ONION: large purplish-red onion.

RIND: zest.

SAFFRON: is available in strands or ground form. It is made from the dried stamens of the crocus flower. The quality varies greatly.

SAMBAL OELEK: a paste made from ground chillies and salt.

SCALLOPS: we used the scallops with coral (roe) attached.

SEASONED PEPPER: a combination of pepper, red pepper, garlic flakes, paprika and natural chicken extract.

SESAME OIL: made from roasted, crushed white sesame seeds. It is always used in small quantities. Do not use for frying.

SNOW PEAS: also known as mange tout (eat all), sugar peas or Chinese peas.

SOY SAUCE: made from fermented soy beans. The light sauce is generally used with white meat for flavour, and the darker variety with red meat for colour. There is a multi-purpose salt-reduced sauce available, also Japanese soy sauce. It is personal taste which sauce you use.

SPAGHETTI SAUCE, BOTTLED: prepared sauce available from supermarkets.

SPATCHCOCK: small chicken weighing about 400g to 500g.

SPINACH (silverbeet): remove coarse white stems, cook green leafy parts as individual recipes indicate.

SPINACH, ENGLISH: a soft-leaved vegetable, more delicate in taste than silverbeet (spinach); however, young silverbeet can be substituted for English spinach.

SPRING ONIONS: vegetables with small white bulbs and long green leaves.

STOCK CUBES: available in beef, chicken or vegetable flavours. If preferred, powdered stock can be used; 1 level teaspoon powdered stock is equivalent to 1 small stock cube.

SUGAR:

We used coarse granulated table sugar, also known as crystal sugar, unless otherwise specified.

Brown: a soft fine-granulated sugar with molasses present which gives colour.

Castor: fine granulated table sugar.

SULTANAS: seedless white raisins.

SWEET AND SOUR SAUCE MIX: powdered product available in packets.

TABASCO SAUCE: made with vinegar, hot red peppers and salt. Use sparingly.

TERIYAKI MARINADE: a blend of soy sauce, wine, vinegar and spices.

TERIYAKI SAUCE: based on the lighter Japanese soy sauce; contains sugar, spices and vinegar.

TOFU: made from boiled, crushed soy beans

to give a type of milk. A coagulant is added, much like the process of cheese making. We used firm tofu in this book. Make sure you buy it as fresh as possible, keep any leftover tofu in the refrigerator under water, which must be changed daily.

TOMATO:

Cherry tomatoes: tom thumb tomatoes, very small and round.

Paste: a concentrated tomato puree used in flavouring soups, stews, sauces, etc.

Puree: is canned, pureed tomatoes (not tomato paste). Use fresh, peeled, pureed tomatoes as a substitute, if preferred.

Sauce: tomato ketchup.

Sun-dried: are dried tomatoes sometimes bottled in oil.

TOMATO SUPREME: a canned product consisting of tomatoes, onions, celery, peppers and seasonings.

TURKEY BREAST ROLL: rolled turkey breast meat.

TURKEY, SMOKED: breast of turkey, cured and delicately smoked.

VEAL:

Topside: boneless piece of meat cut from the leg.

Leg steak: cut from the leg.

Cutlet: cut from the loin.

Schnitzel: cut from the leg.

Steak: cut from the leg.

Medallion: tenderloin or fillet cut from the loin.

VINDALOO CURRY PASTE: thick, Indian seasoning paste with sour-hot flavour. Ingredients are ground chillies, coriander, cumin, fenugreek, mustard, fennel, cinnamon and cloves in a vinegar base.

VINEGAR: we used both white and brown (malt) vinegar in this book.

Balsamic: originated in the province of Modena, Italy. Regional wine is specially processed then aged in antique wooden casks to give pungent flavour.

Rice: a colourless seasoned vinegar containing sugar and salt.

Tarragon: fresh tarragon infused in white wine vinegar.

VEGE-HOT DOGS: vegetarian sausages available from health food stores and some supermarkets.

WINE: we used good quality dry white and red wines.

WORCESTERSHIRE SAUCE: is a spicy sauce used mainly on red meat.

ZUCCHINI: courgette.

Index